STUDY GUIDE

INDIANA CHRISTIAN UNIVERSITY

THE PERSON OF THE HOLY SPIRIT

By
LESTER SUMRALL

LeSEA Publishing Company
P. O. Box 12
South Bend, IN 46624

This special teaching study guide is a college workbook. Space is allowed for your personal notes so the text can grow into your own material.

Audio and video tapes are available to assist you.

All scriptures unless otherwise indicated, are taken from the *New King James Version of the Holy Bible.* Published by Thomas Nelson, Inc., Nashville, Tennessee, 1982.

Scriptures marked *KJV* are taken from the *King James Version of the Holy Bible.*

THE PERSON OF THE HOLY SPIRIT
ISBN 0-937580-83-X

Printed by LESEA PUBLISHING COMPANY, INC.
P. O. Box 12
South Bend, Indiana 46624

STUDY GUIDE

INDIANA CHRISTIAN UNIVERSITY

THE PERSON OF
THE HOLY SPIRIT

TABLE OF CONTENTS

1. An Introduction to the Holy Spirit.. 6

2. The Personhood of the Holy Spirit... 12

3. An Analysis of the Personality of the Holy Spirit........................... 18

4. The Holy Spirit Proceeds from the Father and the Son................... 26

5. The Enemies of the Person of the Holy Spirit................................ 32

6. The Holy Spirit Shared in Creation... 38

7. The Eternal Work of the Holy Spirit 42

8. The Holy Spirit Operated in Mankind Before Christ's Birth 50

9. The Holy Spirit Conceived Jesus Christ 56

10. The Holy Spirit in the Life of Christ.. 64

11. The Work of the Holy Spirit in the Early Church 70

12. The Demands of the Person of the Holy Spirit 76

13. The Sin Against the Person of the Holy Spirit 80

14. The Holy Spirit Intercedes 84

15. The Holy Spirit Imparts Power.. 88

16. The Holy Spirit Reveals the Future 98

17. The Holy Spirit Bestows Gifts on the Church................................ 104

18. The Holy Spirit Bears Fruit 108

19. The Person of the Holy Spirit and the Apostle Paul 116

20. The Person of the Holy Spirit in Romans Eight 122

21. The Holy Spirit in the Book of Revelation 128

22. How to Know and Receive the Person of the Holy Spirit............... 132

INDIANA CHRISTIAN UNIVERSITY

THE PERSON OF THE HOLY SPIRIT

Lesson 1

AN INTRODUCTION TO THE HOLY SPIRIT

INTRODUCTION

The study of the Holy Spirit is one of humanity's highest themes. No truth is as misunderstood, or fought as the Holy Spirit.

There is a universal need and desire for these lessons. The Holy Spirit has come into His own. The time is now!

These studies deal with the Holy Spirit's identity in the Deity. We shall study the Person of the Holy Spirit as God, with all His attributes of personality and idiosyncrasies of rational behavior. We shall see the Holy Spirit on a divine level.

We shall observe that the Holy Spirit is not an abstract dogma of mysticism, nor an impersonal force. The Holy Spirit is not a quality of divine essence.

These studies on the Person of the Holy Spirit are imperative for this generation. One of the greatest needs of the Church is to understand and confront the Third Person of the Trinity.

The Apostles' Creed says, "I believe in the Holy Ghost." A church ignorant of His Person and His mission is ineffective in its world ministry.

Millions of people are aware of the information and fulfillment of need the Holy Spirit can bring to the Church.

He is called the Holy Spirit to reveal that He is not manifested in corporeality. He could also be called "The Holy" or "Holy One."

1. THE SOLE SOURCE OF INFORMATION

A. The Bible is the sole source of information on the Third Person of the Trinity. It is a sufficient source of knowledge.

B. I feel that God the Father, and our Lord Jesus Christ, have spoken to my spirit about the need to better understand the Director of the Dispensation of Grace. We do not need to just talk about Him, but to know Him better. This is especially important during this final dispensation of man's rule on Planet Earth.

Man's rule began with the Dispensation of Innocence in the Garden of Eden and will terminate with the present Dispensation of Grace.

The next dispensation ordained of God is the Kingdom Age, which will have Jesus Christ as its lawgiver and administrator. The Kingdom Dispensation will be ruled by the only Begotten Son, and will last for one thousand years. It is often referred to as the Millennium.

In reality, there are only three dispensations:

1) The Father's Dispensation
2) The Son's Dispensation
3) The Holy Spirit's Dispensation

2. THE HOLY SPIRIT IS NOT A PHANTOM

A. We do not pursue a ghost or a phantom, but a person. He is God the Holy Spirit with all the intricate abilities of His personality.

B. We do not pursue corporeality. The Apostle Paul said that he did not know Jesus in the corporeality of the flesh, but in the Spirit through eternal reality.

II Corinthians 5:16, *Therefore, from now on, we regard no one according to the flesh. Even though we have known Christ according to the flesh, yet now we know Him thus no longer.*

Romans 8:16, 26, *The Spirit Himself bears witness with our spirit that we are children of God.*

v. 26, *Likewise the Spirit also helps in our weaknesses. For we do not know what we should pray for as we ought, but the Spirit Himself makes intercession for us with groanings which cannot be uttered.*

3. THE UNIVERSALITY OF THE HOLY SPIRIT

A. The Holy Spirit is for everyone.

Acts 10:44, *While Peter was still speaking these words, the Holy Spirit fell upon all those who heard the word.*

B. God is not black or white.

John 4:24, *"God is Spirit, and those who worship Him must worship in spirit and truth."*

C. God is light.

I John 1:5, *This is the message which we have heard from Him and declare to you, that God is light and in Him is no darkness at all.*

D. God is fire.

Deuteronomy 4:24, *"For the LORD your God is a consuming fire, a jealous God."*

E. God is love.

I John 4:16, *And we have known and believed the love that God has for us. God is love, and he who abides in love abides in God, and God in him.*

F. The races were created because of sin at the tower of Babel.

8

Genesis 11:9, *Therefore its name is called Babel, because there the LORD confused the language of all the earth; and from there the LORD scattered them abroad over the face of all the earth.*

4. THE THIRD PERSON OF THE TRINITY

I Corinthians 2:12, *Now we have received, not the spirit of the world, but the Spirit who is from God, that we might know the things that have been freely given to us by God.*

The Third Person of the Divine Trinity, the Holy Spirit or Holy Ghost, is preparing the triumphant Church of the Lord Jesus Christ to celebrate the coronation ceremonies of the King of kings! Be ready!

A. Become acquainted with Him.

B. Know Him personally.

C. Become good soil for the planting of eternal truth about the Person of the Holy Spirit.

5. THE WORK OF THE HOLY SPIRIT IN THE NEW TESTAMENT

A. In the gospels, He prophetically established Himself.

B. In the Acts of the Apostles, He directed the new-born Church.

C. In the epistles, He spoke eternal truths in a permanent form.

D. In The Revelation of Jesus Christ, the Holy Spirit operates in divine judgment of the Church, the nations and the devil.

6. HOLY SPIRIT GLORIFIES CHRIST

A. John 16:14, *"He will glorify Me, for He will take of what is Mine and declare it to you."*

One of the chief missions of the Holy Spirit is to glorify Christ, reveal His virtue, His power and His love.

The Holy Spirit is not an alter-ego (other self) of Jesus.

Modernism in theology, especially the denial of the deity of Christ, removes all positive functions of the Holy Spirit from any group. The Holy Spirit is the Spirit of truth.

John 16:13, *"However, when He, the Spirit of truth, has come, He will guide you into all truth; for He will not speak on His own authority, but whatever He hears He will speak; and He will tell you things to come."*

B. The Holy Spirit is the august presence of the Third Person of the Deity, which is His lordship.

We are changed by the Spirit into the image of God.

II Corinthians 3:18, *But we all, with unveiled face, beholding as in a mirror the glory of the Lord, are being transformed into the same image from glory to glory, just as by the Spirit of the Lord.*

False cults are marked by at least one of three errors: another Jesus, another spirit or another gospel.

II Corinthians 11:4, *For if he who comes preaches another Jesus whom we have not preached, or if you receive a different spirit which you have not received, or a different gospel which you have not accepted; you may well put up with it!*

NOTES

THE PERSON OF
THE HOLY SPIRIT

Lesson 2

THE PERSONHOOD OF THE HOLY SPIRIT

INTRODUCTION

Christ said, *"When He is come...."* Divine revelation is called the personhood of the Holy Spirit, the Spirit of truth (John 16:8).

There are 160 listed actions of the Holy Spirit in the Old and New Testaments. Jesus referred to the Holy Spirit as a person 13 times in the gospel of John, chapter 16.

READING

John 16:7-8, *"Nevertheless I tell you the truth. It is to your advantage that I go away; for if I do not go away, the Helper will not come to you; but if I depart, I will send Him to you.*

v. 8, *"And when He has come, He will convict the world of sin, and of righteousness, and of judgment."*

1. THE THIRD ENTITY

The study of the person of God, the Holy Spirit, the third entity of the Divine Trinity, is of tremendous importance to the living Church of Christ today.

The Church needs to know that:

A. The Holy Spirit is not just a blessing to be received.

B. The Holy Spirit is not just an experience.

C. The Holy Spirit is not just an influence.

D. The Holy Spirit is not a neuter gender or an impersonal pronoun—It! He is a proper noun—Holy Spirit.

E. He is a Comforter who feels.

F. He is a Teacher who educates.

G. He is the Guide to follow.

2. THE PERSON OF THE HOLY SPIRIT

A. The Holy Spirit does not speak about Himself, He testifies about Jesus.

John 15:26, *"But when the Helper comes, whom I shall send to you from the Father, the Spirit of truth who proceeds from the Father, He will testify of Me."*

B. He shall glorify Jesus.

John 16:16-17, *"A little while, and you will not see Me; and again a little while, and you will see Me, because I go to the Father."*

v. 17, *Then some of His disciples said among themselves, "What is this that He says to us, 'A little while, and you will not see Me; and again a little while, and you will see Me'; and, 'because I go to the Father'?"*

C. He is the Creator.

D. He is the Convicter.

E. He is the Sealer.

F. He is the Enabler.

G. He is the Comforter.

H. He is the Revealer of divine truth.

I. He is the Builder.

Ephesians 2:20-22, *Having been built on the foundation of the apostles and prophets, Jesus Christ Himself being the chief cornerstone,*

v. 21, *in whom the whole building, being joined together, grows into a holy temple in the Lord,*

v. 22, *in whom you also are being built together for a habitation of God in the Spirit.*

J. The Holy Spirit gives us life.

John 6:63, *"It is the Spirit who gives life; the flesh profits nothing. The words that I speak to you are spirit, and they are life."*

I Peter 3:18, *For Christ also suffered once for sins, the just for the unjust, that He might bring us to God, being put to death in the flesh but made alive by the Spirit.*

K. The Spirit is life.

Revelation 11:11, *Now after the three and a half days the breath of life from God entered them, and they stood on their feet, and great fear fell on those who saw them.*

Zechariah 4:6, *So he answered and said to me: "This is the word of the LORD to Zerubbabel: 'Not by might nor by power, but by My Spirit,' says the LORD of hosts."*

L. The Holy Spirit loves.

Romans 15:30, *Now I beg you, brethren, through the Lord Jesus Christ, and through the love of the Spirit, that you strive together with me in your prayers to God for me.*

M. The Holy Spirit comforts.

Acts 9:31, *Then the churches throughout all Judea, Galilee, and Samaria had peace and were edified. And walking in the fear of the Lord and in the comfort of the Holy Spirit, they were multiplied.*

N. The Holy Spirit possesses a distinct personality with individual attributes.

O. He possesses the total traits of personality.

P. The Holy Spirit does not have an earthly body, or corporeality, like people have.

3. THE HOLY SPIRIT CANNOT BE INSTRUCTED BY MAN

Who can teach the Spirit?

I Corinthians 2:10-11, *But God has revealed them to us through His Spirit. For the Spirit searches all things, yes, the deep things of God.*

v. 11, *For what man knows the things of a man except the spirit of the man which is in him? Even so no one knows the things of God except the Spirit of God.*

Paul's spirit was related to the Holy Spirit; he was anointed to speak by that same Holy Spirit.

4. THE SOULICAL PARTS OF THE HOLY SPIRIT

A. The Holy Spirit has a mind.

Romans 8:27, *Now He who searches the hearts knows what the mind of the Spirit is, because He makes intercession for the saints according to the will of God.*

B. The Holy Spirit has a will.

I Corinthians 12:11, *But one and the same Spirit works all these things, distributing to each one individually as He wills.*

C. The Holy Spirit has emotions.

Isaiah 63:10, *But they rebelled and grieved His Holy Spirit; So He turned Himself against them as an enemy, And He fought against them.*

Grief occurs in the area of emotions.

5. THE HOLY SPIRIT SEARCHES MAN

I Corinthians 2:10, *But God has revealed them to us through His Spirit. For the Spirit searches all things, yes, the deep things of God.*

6. THE HOLY SPIRIT SPEAKS TO CHURCHES

A. The Holy Spirit encourages us to be overcomers. He says, "Do not give up!"

Revelation 2:7, 11, 17, 29, *"He who has an ear, let him hear what the Spirit says to the churches. To him who overcomes I will give to eat from the tree of life, which is in the midst of the Paradise of God."*

v. 11, *"He who has an ear, let him hear what the Spirit says to the churches. He who overcomes shall not be hurt by the second death."*

v. 17, *"He who has an ear, let him hear what the Spirit says to the churches. To him who overcomes I will give some of the hidden manna to eat. And I will give him a white stone, and on* the stone a new name written which no one knows except him who receives it."

v. 29, *"He who has an ear, let him hear what the Spirit says to the churches."*

B. Jesus emphasizes that we should listen to the Holy Spirit.

Revelation 3:6, 13, *"He who has an ear, let him hear what the Spirit says to the churches."*

v. 13, *"He who has an ear, let him hear what the Spirit says to the churches."*

7. THE HOLY SPIRIT AND MAN'S SALVATION

Man's salvation consists of three parts.

A. I John 5:6, *This is He who came by water and blood; Jesus Christ; not only by water, but by water and blood. And it is the Spirit who bears witness, because the Spirit is truth.*

B. I John 5:7, *For there are three that bear witness in heaven: the Father, the Word, and the Holy Spirit; and these three are one.*

8. THE HOLY SPIRIT SANCTIFIES

The Holy Spirit is a vital part of man's salvation.

II Thessalonians 2:13, *But we are bound to give thanks to God always for you, brethren beloved by the Lord, because God from the beginning chose you for salvation through sanctification by the Spirit and belief in the truth.*

THE PERSON OF
THE HOLY SPIRIT

Lesson 3

AN ANALYSIS OF THE PERSONALITY
OF THE HOLY SPIRIT

INTRODUCTION

How do we, as corporeal entities, understand personality? A blind person feels faces in order to recognize people. Your friends and loved ones know the sound of your voice. Some people know you by the way you walk.

READING

I John 4:2, *By this you know the Spirit of God: Every spirit that confesses that Jesus Christ has come in the flesh is of God.*

1. THE PERSON OF THE HOLY SPIRIT

A. The corporeality of man obscures his ability to intimately understand the personality of the Holy Spirit. Man is earthbound. His five senses are materially related.

B. The Holy Spirit is veiled from man's five natural senses. However, every born-again disciple of Jesus Christ has experienced a sense of His presence. Our spirits relate to His Spirit.

Hebrews 10:15, *And the Holy Spirit also witnesses to us...*

I John 5:10, *He who believes in the Son of God has the witness in himself; he who does not believe God has made Him a liar, because he has not believed the testimony that God has given of His Son.*

C. Observe a picture of the Person of the Holy Spirit on the artist's canvas. Prepare the brush and canvas of your spirit. That brush and canvas may open the curtain to reveal the majesty of the Holy Spirit. How does He look?

2. THE HOLY SPIRIT IS THE HEAD OF THIS GENERATION

A leader is in front as a trusted guide.

A. A dog is not a leader–even if he is in front. He obeys his master.

B. A horse is not a leader. He may look or act like one, but the bridle in his mouth means he obeys another master.

3. THE HOLY SPIRIT IS A FAITHFUL GUIDE

God had not left His children helpless, but has provided a guide who knows the way.

John 16:13, *"However, when He, the Spirit of truth, has come, He will guide you into all truth; for He will not speak on His own authority, but whatever He hears He will speak; and He will tell you things to come."*

4. THE HOLY SPIRIT HAS THE FACE OF A JUDGE

The face of a judge is a portrait of equality and justice.

John 16:8, *"And when He has come, He will convict the world of sin, and of righteousness, and of judgment."*

Acts 5:9-11, *Then Peter said to her, "How is it that you have agreed together to test the Spirit of the Lord? Look, the feet of those who have buried your husband are at the door, and they will carry you out."*

v. 10, *Then immediately she fell down at his feet and breathed her last. And the young men came in and found her dead, and carrying her out, buried her by her husband.*

v. 11, *So great fear came upon all the church and upon all who heard these things.*

5. THE HOLY SPIRIT HAS THE FACE OF A TEACHER

A teacher's face is a face of intelligence. It is a beautiful face, a face of wisdom.

Luke 12:12, *"For the Holy Spirit will teach you in that very hour what you ought to say."*

6. THE HOLY SPIRIT HAS THE FACE OF A COMFORTER

The face of the Comforter is one of compassion.

John 14:26, *"But the Helper, the Holy Spirit, whom the Father will send in My name, He will teach you all things, and bring to your remembrance all things that I said to you."*

7. THE HOLY SPIRIT HAS THE FACE OF A COUNSELOR

This is a serene face.

II Corinthians 13:14, *The grace of the Lord Jesus Christ, and the love of God, and the communion of the Holy Spirit be with you all. Amen.*

We receive God's love. We receive Christ's grace. The Holy Spirit counsels, communes and fellowships.

8. THE HOLY SPIRIT HAS A FACE OF STRENGTH

A. The Holy Spirit makes us bold.

Acts 1:8, *"But you shall receive power when the Holy Spirit has come upon you; and you shall be witnesses to Me in Jerusalem, and in all Judea and Samaria, and to the end of the earth."*

B. Jesus was raised from the dead by the Holy Spirit.

Romans 8:11, *But if the Spirit of Him who raised Jesus from the dead dwells in you, He who raised Christ from the dead will also give life to your mortal bodies through His Spirit who dwells in you.*

9. THE HOLY SPIRIT HAS THE FACE OF A LEADER

All disciples can be led by the Spirit. He is our guide to Jesus and the Father.

Romans 8:14, *For as many as are led by the Spirit of God, these are sons of God.*

10. THE HOLY SPIRIT HAS A FACE OF GENEROSITY

He gives great gifts.

I Corinthians 12:1, 8-10, *Now concerning spiritual gifts, brethren, I do not want you to be ignorant.*

v. 8, *For to one is given the word of wisdom through the Spirit, to another the word of knowledge through the same Spirit,*

v. 9, *to another faith by the same Spirit, to another gifts of healings by the same Spirit,*

v. 10, *to another the working of miracles, to another prophecy, to another discerning of spirits, to another different kinds of tongues, to another the interpretation of tongues.*

11. THE HOLY SPIRIT POSSESSES A FACE OF HUMILITY

A. He can be grieved.

Ephesians 4:30, *And do not grieve the Holy Spirit of God, by whom you were sealed for the day of redemption.*

B. He can be resisted.

Acts 7:51, *"You stiffnecked and uncircumcised in heart and ears! You always resist the Holy Spirit; as your fathers did, so do you."*

Imagine divinity and humility united.

12. THE HOLY SPIRIT HAS THE FACE OF ACHIEVEMENT

A. The Holy Spirit was there when the world was created.

B. The Holy Spirit first worked in the cosmos and brought forth continents. Then He began a more difficult work with man.

I Peter 3:18, *For Christ also suffered once for sins, the just for the unjust, that He might bring us to God, being put to death in the flesh but made alive by the Spirit.*

Genesis 6:3, *And the LORD said, "My Spirit shall not strive with man forever, for he is indeed flesh; yet his days shall be one hundred and twenty years."*

13. THE NAMES OF THE HOLY SPIRIT REVEAL HIS PERSONALITY

Names are very important for identification.

A. The Holy Spirit is called the Spirit of God and of Christ.

Romans 8:9, *But you are not in the flesh but in the Spirit, if indeed the Spirit of God dwells in you. Now if anyone does not have the Spirit of Christ, he is not His.*

B. The Holy Spirit is the Revealer of mysteries.

Ephesians 3:4-5, . . .*(By which, when you read, you may understand my knowledge in the mystery of Christ),*

v. 5, *which in other ages was not made known to the sons of men, as it has now been revealed by the Spirit to His holy apostles and prophets.*

1) The Holy Spirit produced the Bible.

Ephesians 6:17, *And take the helmet of salvation, and the sword of the Spirit, which is the word of God.*

2) Holy men anointed by the Spirit wrote the Bible.

II Peter 1:21, *For prophecy never came by the will of man, but holy men of God spoke as they were moved by the Holy Spirit.*

C. He is called the Spirit of wisdom and knowledge. The Bible is the word of the Spirit.

Isaiah 11:2, *The Spirit of the LORD shall rest upon Him, the Spirit of wisdom and understanding, the Spirit of counsel and might, the Spirit of knowledge and of the fear of the LORD.*

I Corinthians 12:8, *For to one is given the word of wisdom through the Spirit, to another the word of knowledge through the same Spirit.*

D. The Spirit of truth

John 14:17, *"Even the Spirit of truth, whom the world cannot receive, because it neither sees Him nor knows Him; but you know Him, for He dwells with you and will be in you."*

E. The Holy Spirit is the power of the Highest. The Holy Spirit brings the Spirit of God to us.

Luke 1:35, *And the angel answered and said to her, "The Holy Spirit will come upon you, and the power of the Highest will overshadow you; therefore, also, that Holy One who is to be born will be called the Son of God.*

Acts 5:3-4, *But Peter said, "Ananias, why has Satan filled your heart to lie to the Holy Spirit and keep back part of the price of the land for yourself?*

v. 4, *"While it remained, was it not your own? And after it was sold, was it not in your own control? Why have you conceived this thing in your heart? You have not lied to men but to God."*

14. THE LOVE OF THE HOLY SPIRIT

The Holy Spirit is a friend.

A. Paul knew the Holy Spirit's love.

Romans 15:30, *Now I beg you, brethren, through the Lord Jesus Christ, and through the love of the Spirit, that you strive together with me in your prayers to God for me.*

B. The Holy Spirit loves us.

Romans 14:17, *For the kingdom of God is not food and drink, but righteousness and peace and joy in the Holy Spirit.*

C. We see His love in teaching and guiding us.

John 14:26, *"But the Helper, the Holy Spirit, whom the Father will send in My name, He will teach you all things, and bring to your remembrance all things that I said to you."*

John 14:13-14, *"And whatever you ask in My name, that I will do, that the Father may be glorified in the Son.*

v. 14, *"If you ask anything in My name, I will do it."*

We see His love in His guidance.

Isaiah 30:21, *Your ears shall hear a word behind you, saying, "This is the way, walk in it," whenever you turn to the right hand or whenever you turn to the left.*

15. THE HOLY SPIRIT DIRECTS OUR WAYS

Acts 8:26, *Now an angel of the Lord spoke to Philip, saying, "Arise and go toward the south along the road which goes down from Jerusalem to Gaza." This is desert.*

16. THE HOLY SPIRIT TEACHES US TO PRAY

Romans 8:26-27, *Likewise the Spirit also helps in our weaknesses. For we do not know what we should pray for as we ought, but the Spirit Himself makes intercession for us with groanings which cannot be uttered.*

v. 27, *Now He who searches the hearts knows what the mind of the Spirit is, because He makes intercession for the saints according to the will of God.*

17. THE HOLY SPIRIT GUARANTEES SPIRITUAL RIGHTS

II Corinthians 1:22, *Who also has sealed us and given us the Spirit in our hearts as a guarantee.*

CONCLUSION

The Holy Spirit feels.
The Holy Spirit thinks.
The Holy Spirit teaches.
The Holy Spirit comforts.

STUDY GUIDE
INDIANA CHRISTIAN UNIVERSITY

THE PERSON OF
THE HOLY SPIRIT

Lesson 4

THE HOLY SPIRIT PROCEEDS FROM
THE FATHER AND THE SON

INTRODUCTION

The Holy Spirit is a person. The purpose of these studies is to reveal His person as a member of the Godhead.

READING

Isaiah 48:16-17, *"Come near to Me, hear this: I have not spoken in secret from the beginning; From the time that it was, I was there. And now the Lord GOD and His Spirit have sent Me."*

v. 17, *Thus says the LORD, your Redeemer, the Holy One of Israel: "I am the LORD your God, who teaches you to profit, who leads you by the way you should go."*

1. THE HOLY SPIRIT IS CALLED GOD

Peter spoke of the Holy Spirit as a person.

Acts 11:7-12, *"And I heard a voice saying to me, 'Rise, Peter; kill and eat.'*

v. 8, *"But I said, 'Not so, Lord! For nothing common or unclean has at any time entered my mouth.'*

v. 9, *"But the voice answered me again from heaven, 'What God has cleansed you must not call common.'*

v. 10, *"Now this was done three times, and all were drawn up again into heaven.*

v. 11, *"At that very moment, three men stood before the house where I was, having been sent to me from Caesarea.*

v. 12, *"Then the Spirit told me to go with them, doubting nothing. Moreover these six brethren accompanied me, and we entered the man's house."*

2. WORSHIP THE FATHER IN THE SPIRIT

John 4:24, *"God is Spirit, and those who worship Him must worship in spirit and truth."*

3. THE HOLY SPIRIT IS PART OF THE TRINITY

I John 5:7-8, *For there are three that bear witness in heaven: the Father, the Word, and the Holy Spirit; and these three are one.*

v. 8, *And there are three that bear witness on earth: the Spirit, the water, and the blood; and these three agree as one.*

4. THE HOLY SPIRIT FILLED CHRIST WITHOUT MEASURE

John 3:34, *"For He whom God has sent speaks the words of God, for God does not give the Spirit by measure."*

John 15:26, *"But when the Helper comes, whom I shall send to you from the Father, the Spirit of truth who proceeds from the Father, He will testify of Me."*

Acts 10:38, *"How God anointed Jesus of Nazareth with the Holy Spirit and with power, who went about doing good and healing all who were oppressed by the devil, for God was with Him."*

5. THE HOLY SPIRIT WORKED WITH THE GODHEAD IN CREATION

Genesis 1:2, *The earth was without form, and void; and darkness was on the face of the deep. And the Spirit of God was hovering over the face of the waters.*

6. THE HOLY SPIRIT WITNESSED JESUS' BAPTISM

Matthew 3:16-17, *Then Jesus, when He had been baptized, came up immediately from the water; and behold, the heavens were opened to Him, and He saw the Spirit of God descending like a dove and alighting upon Him.*

v. 17, *And suddenly a voice came from heaven, saying, "This is My beloved Son, in whom I am well pleased."*

Here we see the functioning together of the Three.

7. THE HOLY SPIRIT TESTIFIES OF CHRIST

John 15:26, *"But when the Helper comes, whom I shall send to you from the Father, the Spirit of truth who proceeds from the Father, He will testify of Me."*

The Three, again, function as one.

8. THE HOLY SPIRIT WORKS WITH THE SON

A. He was sent from the Son.

John 16:7, *"Nevertheless I tell you the truth. It is to your advantage that I go away; for if I do not go away, the Helper will not come to you; but if I depart, I will send Him to you."*

B. He reproves the world.

John 16:8, *"And when He has come, He will convict the world of sin, and of righteousness, and of judgment."*

C. He is the Spirit of truth.

He does not talk about Himself. He relates to us what He hears from the Father and Son.

John 16:13, *"However, when He, the Spirit of truth, has come, He will guide you into all truth; for He will not speak on His own authority, but whatever He hears He will speak; and He will tell you things to come."*

D. He glorifies the Son.

John 16:14, *"He will glorify Me, for He will take of what is Mine and declare it to you."*

9. HE IS THE DIVINE AGENT OF THE GODHEAD

He is omnipotent, omniscient and omnipresent. He is Divinity. The Bible teaches that He is co-equal with the Father and the Son.

Romans 8:9, *But you are not in the flesh but in the Spirit, if indeed the Spirit of God dwells in you. Now if anyone does not have the Spirit of Christ, he is not His.*

10. KNOW HIM

To receive the fullest expression of the Holy Spirit, you must know Him.

A. Knowledge is wisdom.

B. Knowledge is power.

Ephesians 1:17, *That the God of our Lord Jesus Christ, the Father of glory, may give to you the spirit of wisdom and revelation in the knowledge of Him.*

11. FATHER, SON AND HOLY SPIRIT IN THE GREAT COMMISSION

Believers are baptized in the name of the Father, the Son and the Holy Spirit.

Jesus commanded us in Matthew 28:19, *"Go therefore and make disciples of all the nations, baptizing them in the name of the Father and of the Son and of the Holy Spirit."*

12. THE COMMUNION OF THE HOLY SPIRIT

II Corinthians 13:14, *The grace of the Lord Jesus Christ, and the love of God, and the communion of the Holy Spirit be with you all. Amen.*

A. The grace of Jesus

B. The love of God

C. The communion (presence) of the Holy Spirit

13. THE SPIRIT IS CO-EQUAL

He is co-equal in His eternalness.

Hebrews 9:14, *How much more shall the blood of Christ, who through the eternal Spirit offered Himself without spot to God, purge your conscience from dead works to serve the living God?*

14. CHRIST IN THE POWER OF THE SPIRIT

Luke 4:14, *Then Jesus returned in the power of the Spirit to Galilee, and news of Him went out through all the surrounding region.*

15. THE SPIRIT GIVES LIFE

John 6:63, *"It is the Spirit who gives life; the flesh profits nothing. The words that I speak to you are spirit, and they are life."*

16. THE SPIRIT SEARCHES ALL THINGS

The Spirit of God knows what God is thinking.

I Corinthians 2:10, *But God has revealed them to us through His Spirit. For the Spirit searches all things, yes, the deep things of God.*

17. BELIEVERS ARE SEALED WITH THE HOLY SPIRIT

A believer is enclosed or surrounded by the Holy Spirit.

Ephesians 1:13, *In Him you also trusted, after you heard the word of truth, the gospel of your salvation; in whom also, having believed, you were sealed with the Holy Spirit of promise. . .*

STUDY GUIDE

INDIANA CHRISTIAN UNIVERSITY

THE PERSON OF THE HOLY SPIRIT

Lesson 5

THE ENEMIES OF THE PERSON OF THE HOLY SPIRIT

INTRODUCTION

God the Father has enemies. God the Son has enemies. The Person of the Holy Spirit also has enemies.

As God the Father and God the Son have powers of protection, so does the Person of the Holy Spirit.

READING

Psalm 106:32-33, *They angered Him also at the waters of strife, so that it went ill with Moses on account of them;*

v. 33, *Because they rebelled against His Spirit, so that he spoke rashly with his lips.*

Matthew 12:32, *"Anyone who speaks a word against the Son of Man, it will be forgiven him; but whoever speaks against the Holy Spirit, it will not be forgiven him, either in this age or in the age to come."*

1. SATAN

Satan is the Holy Spirit's fiercest enemy. He is the counterfeit of the Holy Spirit.

I John 4:3, *And every spirit that does not confess that Jesus Christ has come in the flesh is not of God. And this is the spirit of the Anti-christ, which you have heard was coming, and is now already in the world.*

2. DEMONS

We can test which spirits are demonic and which are of God.

I John 4:1-2, *Beloved, do not believe every spirit, but test the spirits, whether they are of God; because many false prophets have gone out into the world.*

v. 2, *By this you know the Spirit of God: Every spirit that confesses that Jesus Christ has come in the flesh is of God.*

Matthew 12:43-45, *"When an unclean spirit goes out of a man, he goes through dry places, seeking rest, and finds none.*

v. 44, *"Then he says, 'I will return to my house from which I came.' And when he comes, he finds it empty, swept, and put in order.*

v. 45, *"Then he goes and takes with him seven other spirits more wicked than himself, and they enter and dwell there; and the last state of that man is worse than the first. So shall it also be with this wicked generation."*

3. THE WORLD REFUSES SANCTIFICATION

Unbelievers do not want to live holy lives. They hate having their wicked deeds exposed.

I Peter 1:2, *Elect according to the foreknowledge of God the Father, in sanctification of the Spirit, for obedience and sprinkling of the blood of Jesus Christ: Grace to you and peace be multiplied.*

II Thessalonians 2:13, *But we are bound to give thanks to God always for you, brethren beloved by the Lord, because God from the beginning chose you for salvation through sanctification by the Spirit and belief in the truth.*

I Thessalonians 5:19, *Do not quench the Spirit.*

4. THE WORLD OPPOSES FREEDOM OF WORSHIP

The world hates happy Christians.

John 15:19, *"If you were of the world, the world would love its own. Yet because you are not of the world, but I chose you out of the world, therefore the world hates you."*

5. THE FLESH LUSTS AGAINST THE SPIRIT

A. The Spirit of God demands that we control the desires of the flesh.

Ephesians 2:3, *Among whom also we all once conducted ourselves in the lusts of our flesh, fulfilling the desires of the flesh and of the mind, and were by nature children of wrath, just as the others.*

Acts 7:51, *"You stiffnecked and uncircumcised in heart and ears! You always resist the Holy Spirit; as your fathers did, so do you."*

B. God's Spirit dwells in the believer.

Romans 8:9, *But you are not in the flesh but in the Spirit, if indeed the Spirit of God dwells in you. Now if anyone does not have the Spirit of Christ, he is not His.*

C. There is constant warfare between the flesh and the Spirit.

Galatians 5:17, *For the flesh lusts against the Spirit, and the Spirit against the flesh; and these are contrary to one another, so that you do not do the things that you wish.*

Galatians 6:8, *For he who sows to his flesh will of the flesh reap corruption, but he who sows to the Spirit will of the Spirit reap everlasting life.*

D. We have a new relationship in Christ.

II Corinthians 5:16-17, *Therefore, from now on, we regard no one according to the flesh. Even though we have known Christ according to the flesh, yet now we know Him thus no longer.*

v. 17, *Therefore, if anyone is in Christ, he is a new creation; old things have passed away; behold, all things have become new.*

6. FALSE RELIGIONS

False religions are the enemies of the Holy Spirit, because He is the Spirit of truth who exalts Jesus.

John 16:13-14, *"However, when He, the Spirit of truth, has come, He will guide you into all truth; for He will not speak on His own authority, but whatever He hears He will speak; and He will tell you things to come.*

v. 14, *"He will glorify Me, for He will take of what is Mine and declare it to you."*

7. THE HOLY SPIRIT CAN BE GRIEVED

The Holy Spirit is sensitive.

Ephesians 4:30, *And do not grieve the Holy Spirit of God, by whom you were sealed for the day of redemption.*

8. THE HOLY SPIRIT CAN BE QUENCHED

The quenching of the Spirit is a function of soulical emotions.

I Thessalonians 5:19, *Do not quench the Spirit.*

9. THE HOLY SPIRIT CAN BE VEXED

When Israel rebelled against the will and purpose of God, this vexed His Holy Spirit.

"To vex" means "to give trouble to, especially in a petty or nagging way; to disturb, annoy, irritate; to distress, afflict or plague; to keep bringing up, going over, or returning to a matter difficult to solve; to shake or toss about."

Isaiah 63:10, *But they rebelled, and vexed his holy Spirit: therefore he was turned to be their enemy, and he fought against them.* (KJV)

10. THE HOLY SPIRIT CAN BE PROVOKED

It was Israel's rebellion against God and God's servant Moses which provoked Him.

Isaiah 65:2-3, *I have stretched out My hands all day long to a rebellious people, who walk in a way that is not good, according to their own thoughts;*

v. 3, *A people who provoke Me to anger continually to My face; who sacrifice in gardens, and burn incense on altars of brick.*

11. THE HOLY SPIRIT CAN BE RESISTED

Acts 7:51, *"You stiffnecked and uncircumcised in heart and ears! You always resist the Holy Spirit; as your fathers did, so do you."*

12. YOU CAN LIE TO THE HOLY SPIRIT

Acts 5:3-4, *But Peter said, "Ananias, why has Satan filled your heart to lie to the Holy Spirit and keep back part of the price of the land for yourself?*

v. 4, *"While it remained, was it not your own? And after it was sold, was it not in your own control? Why have you conceived this thing in your heart? You have not lied to men but to God."*

Cooperate with His activities. Realize His plan for your life. Experience the fullness of His majesty by doing natural things spiritually.

The Holy Spirit challenges the spirit of this age!

NOTES

_____
_____
_____
_____
_____
_____
_____
_____
_____
_____
_____
_____
_____
_____
_____
_____
_____
_____
_____
_____
_____
_____
_____
_____
_____
_____
_____
_____
_____
_____

INDIANA CHRISTIAN UNIVERSITY

THE PERSON OF
THE HOLY SPIRIT

Lesson 6

THE HOLY SPIRIT SHARED IN CREATION

INTRODUCTION

The Holy Spirit shared in the creation of Earth. The Hebrew word, *Elohim* is a plural term. It means more than one, and signifies the Trinity. *The LORD God* is a singular phrase, but is used to translate the plural word, *Elohim*. Therefore, the Holy Spirit was present at the creation of:

A. The heavens and earth

Genesis 2:4, *This is the history of the heavens and the earth when they were created, in the day that the LORD God made the earth and the heavens.*

B. Man

Genesis 1:26, *Then God said, "Let Us make man in Our image, according to Our likeness; let them have dominion over the fish of the sea, over the birds of the air, and over the cattle, over all the earth and over every creeping thing that creeps on the earth."*

Genesis 2:7, *And the LORD God formed man of the dust of the ground, and breathed into his nostrils the breath of life; and man became a living being.*

C. The Garden of Eden

Genesis 2:8, *The LORD God planted a garden eastward in Eden, and there He put the man whom He had formed.*

D. The animal kingdom

Genesis 2:19, *Out of the ground the LORD God formed every beast of the field and every bird of the air, and brought them to Adam to see what he would call them. And whatever Adam called each living creature, that was its name.*

E. Woman

Genesis 2:22, *Then the rib which the LORD God had taken from man He made into a woman, and He brought her to the man.*

READING

Genesis 1:1-2, *In the beginning God created the heavens and the earth.*

v. 2, *The earth was without form, and void; and darkness was on the face of the deep. And the Spirit of God was hovering over the face of the waters.*

1. THE FIRST REVELATION OF GOD, THE HOLY SPIRIT

The Spirit of God used a confused mass of matter; void, empty, dark and without form. The Holy Spirit moved and changed chaos into creation!

Psalm 33:6, *By the word of the LORD the heavens were made, and all the host of them by the breath of His mouth.*

Job 26:13, *By His Spirit He adorned the heavens; His hand pierced the fleeing serpent.*

2. THE HOLY SPIRIT WORKED WITH THE ANTE-DILUVIANS

The Holy Spirit works with the Father to turn mankind around. He strives with men.

Genesis 6:3, *And the LORD said, My Spirit shall not strive with man forever, for he is indeed flesh; yet his days shall be one hundred and twenty years.*

3. THE HOLY SPIRIT MOVES IN WORLD REDEMPTION

The blood of Christ was presented to God by the Holy Spirit.

Hebrews 9:14, *How much more shall the blood of Christ, who through the eternal Spirit offered Himself without spot to God, purge your conscience from dead works to serve the living God?*

4. THE HOLY SPIRIT WORKS IN THE NEW BIRTH

Mankind can birth a body, but the Spirit can birth spirit.

John 3:5-8, *Jesus answered, "Most assuredly, I say to you, unless one is born of water and the Spirit, he cannot enter the kingdom of God.*

v. 6, *That which is born of the flesh is flesh, and that which is born of the Spirit is spirit.*

v. 7, *Do not marvel that I said to you, 'You must be born again.'*

v. 8, *The wind blows where it wishes, and you hear the sound of it, but cannot tell where it comes from and where it goes. So is everyone who is born of the Spirit."*

John 6:63, *"It is the Spirit who gives life; the flesh profits nothing. The words that I speak to you are spirit, and they are life."*

NOTES

_____

_____

_____

_____

_____

_____

_____

_____

_____

_____

_____

_____

_____

_____

_____

_____

_____

_____

_____

_____

_____

_____

_____

_____

_____

_____

_____

_____

_____

_____

_____

_____

_____

_____

_____

_____

_____

_____

_____

_____

_____

THE PERSON OF
THE HOLY SPIRIT

Lesson 7

THE ETERNAL WORKS OF THE HOLY SPIRIT

READING

John 14:17, *"Even the Spirit of truth, whom the world cannot receive, because it neither sees Him nor knows Him; but you know Him, for He dwells with you and will be in you."*

1. THE HOLY SPIRIT IS THE ETERNAL

We have no biblical reference to His beginning. The Bible never tries to prove His existence.

Hebrews 9:14, *How much more shall the blood of Christ, who through the eternal Spirit offered Himself without spot to God, purge your conscience from dead works to serve the living God?*

He was not created. Eternal means, "without a beginning or end of existence."

The Holy Spirit is not just an influence. An influence has no power to determine, decide, think, or teach. An influence has no power to act, perform, or shake a building.

Acts 4:31, *And when they had prayed, the place where they were assembled together was shaken; and they were all filled with the Holy Spirit, and they spoke the word of God with boldness.*

If the Holy Spirit is God, He must be recognized as a person of the Godhead, and glorified as God.

2. THREE TIME PERIODS IN REFERENCE TO THE GODHEAD

A. Man's time on planet Earth can be divided into three time periods in reference to the Godhead.

    1) God the Father–the Old Testament.

    2) God the Son–the four gospels.

    3) God the Holy Spirit–the Acts of the Apostles, epistles and The Revelation of Jesus Christ.

B. The Holy Spirit was with God the Father throughout the Old Testament.

Genesis 1:2, *The earth was without form, and void; and darkness was on the face of the deep. And the Spirit of God was hovering over the face of the waters.*

C. The Holy Spirit worked in the earthly life of Jesus.

    1) At His birth

Luke 1:35, *And the angel answered and said to her, "The Holy Spirit will come upon you, and the power of the Highest will overshadow you; therefore, also, that Holy One who is to be born will be called the Son of God."*

    2) At His baptism

Mark 1:9-10, *It came to pass in those days that Jesus came from Nazareth of Galilee, and was baptized by John in the Jordan.*

v. 10, *And immediately, coming up from the water, He saw the heavens parting and the Spirit descending upon Him like a dove.*

3. THE SPIRIT IS ETERNAL TRUTH

A. I John 5:6, *This is He who came by water and blood—Jesus Christ; not only by water, but by water and blood. And it is the Spirit who bears witness, because the Spirit is truth.*

B. The Spirit of God within us helps us discern between truth and error.

I John 4:6, *We are of God. He who knows God hears us; he who is not of God does not hear us. By this we know the spirit of truth and the spirit of error.*

C. The Holy Spirit draws our attention to Jesus.

John 16:13, *"However, when He, the Spirit of truth, has come, He will guide you into all truth; for He will not speak on His own authority, but whatever He hears He will speak; and He will tell you things to come."*

4. THE HOLY SPIRIT PROVIDES ETERNAL ACCESS TO THE THRONE ROOM OF GOD

The Holy Spirit can lead us into the presence of the Father.

Ephesians 2:18, *For through Him we both have access by one Spirit to the Father.*

Galatians 5:18, *But if you are led by the Spirit, you are not under the law.*

5. THE ETERNAL HOLY SPIRIT IS UNSEARCHABLE BY HUMAN WISDOM

No one can teach the Spirit. The seven Spirits of God are the fullness of all His attributes.

I Corinthians 2:11, *For what man knows the things of a man except the spirit of the man which is in him? Even so no one knows the things of God except the Spirit of God.*

Revelation 5:6, *And I looked, and behold, in the midst of the throne and of the four living creatures, and in the midst of the elders, stood a Lamb as though it had been slain, having seven horns and seven eyes, which are the seven Spirits of God sent out into all the earth.*

6. THE OMNIPOTENCE OF THE ETERNAL HOLY SPIRIT

God the Holy Spirit has existed throughout eternity. He is an omnipotent force. He has eternal, unlimited power.

A. The Holy Spirit raised Jesus from the dead.

I Peter 3:18, *For Christ also suffered once for sins, the just for the unjust, that He might bring us to God, being put to death in the flesh but made alive by the Spirit.*

B. The Holy Spirit gives us constant and eternal renewal. Even a man's body is renewed when the Holy Spirit lives within him.

Romans 8:11, *But if the Spirit of Him who raised Jesus from the dead dwells in you, He who raised Christ from the dead will also give life to your mortal bodies through His Spirit who dwells in you.*

C. The Holy Spirit eternally works signs and wonders.

Romans 15:19, *In mighty signs and wonders, by the power of the Spirit of God, so that from Jerusalem and round about to Illyricum I have fully preached the gospel of Christ.*

Hebrews 2:3-4, *How shall we escape if we neglect so great a salvation, which at the first began to be spoken by the Lord, and was confirmed to us by those who heard Him,*

v. 4, *God also bearing witness both with signs and wonders, with various miracles, and gifts of the Holy Spirit, according to His own will?*

D. The eternal Holy Spirit makes the believer abound in hope.

Romans 15:13, *Now may the God of hope fill you with all joy and peace in believing, that you may abound in hope by the power of the Holy Spirit.*

7. THE ETERNAL SPIRIT IS OMNISCIENT

The Holy Spirit is omniscient, with unlimited knowledge. He can reveal what man has not seen.

I Corinthians 2:10, *But God has revealed them to us through His Spirit. For the Spirit searches all things, yes, the deep things of God.*

8. THE OMNIPRESENCE OF THE HOLY SPIRIT

The Holy Spirit is omnipresent; He has the ability to be present in all places all the time.

Psalm 139:7-10, *Where can I go from Your Spirit? Or where can I flee from Your presence?*

v. 8, *If I ascend into heaven, You are there; If I make my bed in hell, behold, You are there.*

v. 9, *If I take the wings of the morning, and dwell in the uttermost parts of the sea,*

v. 10, *Even there Your hand shall lead me, and Your right hand shall hold me.*

9. THE ETERNAL SPIRIT AND ETERNAL WORD ARE ONE

The Holy Spirit dictated the Bible.

II Peter 1:21, *For prophecy never came by the will of man, but holy men of God spoke as they were moved by the Holy Spirit.*

10. THE HOLY SPIRIT IS AN ETERNAL INSTRUCTOR

A. The Holy Spirit teaches believers to look at things from a spiritual, rather than a carnal viewpoint.

I Corinthians 2:13, *These things we also speak, not in words which man's wisdom teaches but which the Holy Spirit teaches, comparing spiritual things with spiritual.*

B. The eternal Word is the Holy Spirit.

Ephesians 6:17, *And take the helmet of salvation, and the sword of the Spirit, which is the word of God.*

11. JESUS WAS CONCEIVED BY THE ETERNAL SPIRIT

A. The eternal Spirit had a very real part in Christ's natural birth.

Matthew 1:20, *But while he thought about these things, behold, an angel of the Lord appeared to him in a dream, saying, "Joseph, son of David, do not be afraid to take to you Mary your wife, for that which is conceived in her is of the Holy Spirit."*

B. The eternal Spirit anointed Jesus Christ for His ministry.

Luke 4:18, *"The Spirit of the LORD is upon Me, because He has anointed Me to preach the gospel to the poor. He has sent Me to heal the brokenhearted, to proclaim liberty to the captives and recovery of sight to the blind, to set at liberty those who are oppressed."*

C. The eternal Spirit anointed Jesus Christ for the deliverance of mankind.

Acts 10:38, *"How God anointed Jesus of Nazareth with the Holy Spirit and with power, who went about doing good and healing all who were oppressed by the devil, for God was with Him."*

D. The eternal Spirit anointed Jesus to teach.

Acts 1:1, *The former account I made, O Theophilus, of all that Jesus began both to do and teach.*

E. The eternal Spirit anointed God's servants for ministry.

Acts 1:2, *Until the day in which He was taken up, after He through the Holy Spirit had given commandments to the apostles whom He had chosen.*

12. THE ETERNAL SPIRIT PROPHESIED CHRIST'S COMING KINGDOM

Isaiah 9:7, *Of the increase of His government and peace there will be no end, upon the throne of David and over His kingdom, to order it and establish it with judgment and justice from that time forward, even forever. The zeal of the LORD of hosts will perform this.*

13. THE ETERNAL SPIRIT BIRTHS EVERY TRUE CHRISTIAN

John 3:5, *Jesus answered, "Most assuredly, I say to you, unless one is born of water and the Spirit, he cannot enter the kingdom of God."*

14. THE HOLY SPIRIT MAKES EVERY CHRISTIAN A TEMPLE

I Corinthians 6:19-20, *Or do you not know that your body is the temple of the Holy Spirit who is in you, whom you have from God, and you are not your own?*

v. 20, *For you were bought at a price; therefore glorify God in your body and in your spirit, which are God's.*

15. THE ETERNAL SPIRIT MAKES ALIVE

Romans 8:9-11, *But you are not in the flesh but in the Spirit, if indeed the Spirit of God dwells in you. Now if anyone does not have the Spirit of Christ, he is not His.*

v. 10, *And if Christ is in you, the body is dead because of sin, but the Spirit is life because of righteousness.*

v. 11, *But if the Spirit of Him who raised Jesus from the dead dwells in you, He who raised Christ from the dead will also give life to your mortal bodies through His Spirit who dwells in you.*

16. WALK IN THE ETERNAL SPIRIT FOR TOTAL VICTORY

Galatians 5:16, *I say then: Walk in the Spirit, and you shall not fulfill the lust of the flesh.*

NOTES

_____

_____

_____

_____

_____

_____

_____

_____

_____

_____

_____

_____

_____

_____

_____

_____

_____

_____

_____

_____

_____

_____

_____

_____

_____

_____

_____

_____

THE PERSON OF
THE HOLY SPIRIT

Lesson 8

THE HOLY SPIRIT OPERATED IN MANKIND
BEFORE CHRIST'S BIRTH

INTRODUCTION

The Holy Spirit has operated in man since Adam. In the Old Testament, the Holy Spirit worked through men as the occasion demanded it. In the New Testament, the Holy Spirit worked in men by dwelling within them. The Holy Spirit still operates this way today!

READING

Zechariah 4:6, *So he answered and said to me: "This is the word of the LORD to Zerubbabel: 'Not by might nor by power, but by My Spirit,' says the LORD of hosts."*

1. THE HOLY SPIRIT'S DEBUT ON PLANET EARTH

A. Genesis 1:2, *The earth was without form, and void; and darkness was on the face of the deep. And the Spirit of God was hovering over the face of the waters.*

B. Genesis 6:3, *And the LORD said, "My Spirit shall not strive with man forever, for he is indeed flesh; yet his days shall be one hundred and twenty years."*

2. THE HOLY SPIRIT WORKED THROUGH JOSEPH

Pharaoh recognized the Spirit of God in Joseph.

Genesis 41:38-40, *And Pharaoh said to his servants, "Can we find such a one as this, a man in whom is the Spirit of God?"*

v. 39, *Then Pharaoh said to Joseph, "Inasmuch as God has shown you all this, there is no one as discerning and wise as you.*

v. 40, *"You shall be over my house, and all my people shall be ruled according to your word; only in regard to the throne will I be greater than you."*

3. THE SEVENTY ELDERS OF ISRAEL

The same Spirit upon Moses was passed to many others.

Numbers 11:25, *Then the LORD came down in the cloud, and spoke to him, and took of the Spirit that was upon him, and placed the same upon the seventy elders; and it happened, when the Spirit rested upon them, that they prophesied, although they never did so again.*

4. MOSES LAID HANDS ON JOSHUA

The Lord divinely commanded Moses to bless Joshua.

Deuteronomy 34:9, *Now Joshua the son of Nun was full of the spirit of wisdom, for Moses had laid his hands on him; so the children of Israel heeded him, and did as the LORD had commanded Moses.*

5. BEZALEEL WAS FILLED WITH THE SPIRIT OF GOD

Bezaleel did much of the creative work for the tabernacle. He was given supernatural power to do a natural work.

Exodus 31:3, *"And I have filled him with the Spirit of God, in wisdom, in understanding, in knowledge, and in all manner of workmanship."*

6. GIDEON RECEIVED THE SPIRIT

Judges 6:34, *But the Spirit of the LORD came upon Gideon; then he blew the trumpet, and the Abiezrites gathered behind him.*

7. THE HOLY SPIRIT WORKED IN SAMSON

Samson received supernatural strength from the Holy Spirit.

Judges 15:14-15, *When he came to Lehi, the Philistines came shouting against him. Then the Spirit of the LORD came mightily upon him; and the ropes that were on his arms became like flax that is burned with fire, and his bonds broke loose from his hands.*

v. 15, *He found a fresh jawbone of a donkey, reached out his hand and took it, and killed a thousand men with it.*

8. THE HOLY SPIRIT FELL UPON DAVID

David became a changed man after he was anointed.

I Samuel 16:13, *Then Samuel took the horn of oil and anointed him in the midst of his brothers; and the Spirit of the LORD came upon David from that day forward. So Samuel arose and went to Ramah.*

9. THE HOLY SPIRIT WORKED THROUGH DANIEL

Daniel 4:8, *But at last Daniel came before me (his name is Belteshazzar, according to the name of my god; in him is the Spirit of the Holy God), and I told the dream before him, saying. . .*

Daniel 4:18, *"This dream I, King Nebuchadnezzar, have seen. Now you, Belteshazzar, declare its interpretation, since all the wise men of my kingdom are not able to make known to me the interpretation; but you are able, for the Spirit of the Holy God is in you."*

10. DANIEL SAW THE TRINITY

Daniel had a vision of the eternal Son of Man, carried by the Spirit to the throne of the Ancient of Days.

Daniel 7:13-14, *"I was watching in the night visions, And behold, One like the Son of Man, coming with the clouds of heaven! He came to the Ancient of Days, and they brought Him near before Him.*

v. 14, *Then to Him was given dominion and glory and a kingdom, that all peoples, nations, and languages should serve Him. His dominion is an everlasting dominion, which shall not pass away, and His kingdom the one which shall not be destroyed."*

11. EZEKIEL PROPHESIED ABOUT THE HOLY SPIRIT

Ezekiel 36:27, *"I will put My Spirit within you and cause you to walk in My statutes, and you will keep My judgments and do them."*

12. MICAH WAS USED BY THE HOLY SPIRIT

Micah was used as a mouthpiece by the Spirit to convict Israel of sin.

Micah 3:8, *But truly I am full of power by the Spirit of the LORD, and of justice and might, to declare to Jacob his transgression and to Israel his sin.*

13. THE PROPHET HAGGAI

Haggai assured Israel that God's Spirit would not leave them.

Haggai 2:5, *"According to the word that I covenanted with you when you came out of Egypt, so My Spirit remains among you; do not fear!"*

14. THE HOLY SPIRIT WORKED WITH ELIZABETH

The spirit of the unborn baby in Elizabeth responded to the Spirit of Mary's unborn baby.

Luke 1:41-45, *And it happened, when Elizabeth heard the greeting of Mary, that the babe leaped in her womb; and Elizabeth was filled with the Holy Spirit.*

v. 42, *Then she spoke out with a loud voice and said, "Blessed are you among women, and blessed is the fruit of your womb!*

v. 43, *"But why is this granted to me, that the mother of my Lord should come to me?*

v. 44, *"For indeed, as soon as the voice of your greeting sounded in my ears, the babe leaped in my womb for joy.*

v. 45, *"Blessed is she who believed, for there will be a fulfillment of those things which were told her from the Lord."*

15. THE HOLY SPIRIT USED ZACHARIAS

When Zacharias declared that his son's name was John rather than Zacharias, his tongue was loosened by the Holy Spirit.

Luke 1:62-63, 65, *So they made signs to his father; what he would have him called.*

v. 63, *And he asked for a writing tablet, and wrote, saying, "His name is John." So they all marveled.*

v. 65, *Then fear came on all who dwelt around them; and all these sayings were discussed throughout all the hill country of Judea.*

16. THE SPIRIT OF CHRIST WAS PROPHESIED

A. Isaiah 11:2, *The Spirit of the LORD shall rest upon Him, the Spirit of wisdom and understanding, the Spirit of counsel and might, the Spirit of knowledge and of the fear of the LORD.*

B. Isaiah 61:1, *"The Spirit of the Lord GOD is upon Me, because the LORD has anointed Me to preach good tidings to the poor; He has sent Me to heal the brokenhearted, to proclaim liberty to the captives, and the opening of the prison to those who are bound."*

NOTES

_____

_____

_____

_____

_____

_____

_____

_____

_____

_____

_____

_____

_____

_____

_____

_____

_____

_____

_____

_____

_____

_____

_____

_____

_____

_____

_____

_____

_____

_____

_____

_____

THE PERSON OF
THE HOLY SPIRIT

Lesson 9

THE HOLY SPIRIT CONCEIVED
JESUS CHRIST

INTRODUCTION

There are tender and mysterious functions of the Person of the Holy Spirit. He works in nature and nations.

The variety of activities of the Person of the Holy Spirit is amazing. One of the greatest controversies of all time is over the virgin-born Son of Mary, in which the Holy Spirit had a part.

Religious leaders throughout the world have claimed to have been born to a virgin, but those claims have only proven to be legends. No person can ever fathom the depth of God's operation, and the conception of His Son, the Lord Jesus Christ.

READING

Matthew 1:20, *But while he thought about these things, behold, an angel of the Lord appeared to him in a dream, saying, "Joseph, son of David, do not be afraid to take to you Mary your wife, for that which is conceived in her is of the Holy Spirit."*

1. REMEMBER WHAT GOD HAS DONE!

A. Paul said, "Fourteen years ago I knew a man."

B. Moses wandered in the desert for forty years before he received a manifestation of God.

2. A WOMAN AND TOWN CHOSEN BY THE SPIRIT

A. Isaiah called Mary a virgin.

Isaiah 7:14, *"Therefore the Lord Himself will give you a sign: Behold, the virgin shall conceive and bear a Son, and shall call His name Immanuel."*

Matthew 1:22-23 (fulfillment), *So all this was done that it might be fulfilled which was spoken by the Lord through the prophet, saying:*

v. 23, *"Behold, the virgin shall be with child, and bear a Son, and they shall call His name Immanuel,"* which is translated, *"God with us."*

B. Nazareth was chosen as this special town.

Luke 1:26, *Now in the sixth month the angel Gabriel was sent by God to a city of Galilee named Nazareth.*

3. THE ROMAN WORLD WAS PREPARED POLITICALLY

Luke 2:1-5, *And it came to pass in those days that a decree went out from Caesar Augustus that all the world should be registered.*

v. 2, *This census first took place while Quirinius was governing Syria.*

v. 3, *So all went to be registered, everyone to his own city.*

v. 4, *And Joseph also went up from Galilee, out of the city of Nazareth, into Judea, to the city of David, which is called Bethlehem, because he was of the house and lineage of David,*

v. 5, *to be registered with Mary, his betrothed wife, who was with child.*

4. THE HOLY SPIRIT REVEALED THE EVENT

A. Simeon

Luke 2:25-32, *And behold, there was a man in Jerusalem whose name was Simeon, and this man was just and devout, waiting for the Consolation of Israel, and the Holy Spirit was upon him.*

v. 26, *And it had been revealed to him by the Holy Spirit that he would not see death before he had seen the Lord's Christ.*

v. 27, *So he came by the Spirit into the temple. And when the parents brought in the Child Jesus, to do for Him according to the custom of the law,*

v. 28, *he took Him up in his arms and blessed God and said:*

v. 29. *"Lord, now You are letting Your servant depart in peace, According to Your word;*

v. 30, *For my eyes have seen Your salvation*

v. 31, *Which You have prepared before the face of all peoples,*

v. 32, *A light to bring revelation to the Gentiles, and the glory of Your people Israel."*

B. Anna

Luke 2:36-38, *Now there was one, Anna, a prophetess, the daughter of Phanuel, of the tribe of Asher. She was of a great age, and had lived with a husband seven years from her virginity;*

v. 37, and this woman was a widow of about eighty-four years, who did not depart from the temple, but served God with fastings and prayers night and day.

v. 38, And coming in that instant she gave thanks to the Lord, and spoke of Him to all those who looked for redemption in Jerusalem.

5. JESUS' BIRTH WAS A BIOLOGICAL MIRACLE

Mary was impregnated by the Holy Spirit.

Matthew 1:18, 23, *Now the birth of Jesus Christ was as follows: After His mother Mary was betrothed to Joseph, before they came together, she was found with child of the Holy Spirit.*

v. 23, "Behold, the virgin shall be with child, and bear a Son, and they shall call His name Immanuel," which is translated, "God with us."

6. THE NEWS WAS ANNOUNCED BY AN ANGEL

It happened in a provincial town where neighbors said, "Can any good thing come out of Nazareth?" The conception of Jesus Christ was a test of faith.

Luke 1:35, *And the angel answered and said to her, "The Holy Spirit will come upon you, and the power of the Highest will overshadow you; therefore, also, that Holy One who is to be born will be called the Son of God."*

7. THE IDEA OF THE IMMACULATE BIRTH CAME FROM THE HOLY SPIRIT

A. The Christ, Son of God, would come from the House of David.

Isaiah 9:6-7, *For unto us a Child is born, unto us a Son is given; And the government will be upon His shoulder. And His name will be called Wonderful, Counselor, Mighty God, Everlasting Father, Prince of Peace.*

v. 7, *Of the increase of His government and peace there will be no end, upon the throne of David and over His kingdom, to order it and establish it with judgment and justice from that time forward, even forever. The zeal of the LORD of hosts will perform this.*

B. Galatians 4:4, *But when the fullness of the time had come, God sent forth His Son, born of a woman, born under the law.*

God is ALWAYS on time!

8. THE HOLY SPIRIT ASSURES TOTAL VICTORY

A. The angel told Mary not to be afraid.

Luke 1:30, *Then the angel said to her, "Do not be afraid, Mary, for you have found favor with God."*

B. The Spirit came to Moses.

Exodus 3:2, *And the Angel of the LORD appeared to him in a flame of fire from the midst of a bush. So he looked, and behold, the bush was burning with fire, but the bush was not consumed.*

C. The Spirit took Elijah.

II Kings 2:9, 14, *And so it was, when they had crossed over, that Elijah said to Elisha, "Ask! What may I do for you, before I am taken away from you?" Elisha said, "Please let a double portion of your spirit be upon me."*

v. 14, *Then he took the mantle of Elijah that had fallen from him, and struck the water, and said, "Where is the LORD God of Elijah?" And when he also had struck the water, it was divided this way and that; and Elisha crossed over.*

D. The Spirit spoke to Daniel.

Daniel 10:5, 10-12, *I lifted my eyes and looked, and behold, a certain man clothed in linen, whose waist was girded with gold of Uphaz!*

v. 10, *Then, suddenly, a hand touched me, which made me tremble on my knees and on the palms of my hands.*

v. 11, *And he said to me, "O Daniel, man greatly beloved, understand the words that I speak to you, and stand upright, for I have now been sent to you." While he was speaking this word to me, I stood trembling.*

v. 12, *Then he said to me, "Do not fear, Daniel, for from the first day that you set your heart to understand, and to humble yourself before your God, your words were heard; and I have come because of your words."*

9. THE HOLY ONE...THE SON OF GOD

Luke 1:35, *And the angel answered and said to her, "The Holy Spirit will come upon you, and the power of the Highest will overshadow you; therefore, also, that Holy One who is to be born will be called the Son of God."*

A. "Unique" seems so inadequate when describing the greatest birth in history.

B. The angels proclaimed the arrival of the world's Savior over the hills of Bethlehem in Luke 2:8-14.

They proclaimed peace.

Luke 2:14, *"Glory to God in the highest, And on earth peace, good will toward men!"*

The shepherds were afraid of the supernatural phenomenon.

Luke 2:9, *And behold, an angel of the Lord stood before them, and the glory of the Lord shone around them, and they were greatly afraid.*

C. The cosmos shook, and a star guided three unusual men from Persia to see the astounding miracle.

Matthew 2:1, *Now after Jesus was born in Bethlehem of Judea in the days of Herod the king, behold, wise men from the East came to Jerusalem.*

10. THIS WORK OF THE HOLY SPIRIT

A. Profound explanations

B. Divine operations

C. World-changing consummation

D. There is hope for all humanity in His realization.

NOTES

_____
_____
_____
_____
_____
_____
_____
_____
_____
_____
_____
_____
_____
_____
_____
_____
_____
_____
_____
_____
_____
_____
_____
_____
_____
_____
_____
_____
_____
_____
_____
_____
_____
_____

STUDY GUIDE

INDIANA CHRISTIAN UNIVERSITY

THE PERSON OF THE HOLY SPIRIT

Lesson 10

THE HOLY SPIRIT IN THE LIFE OF CHRIST

INTRODUCTION

No life on earth has been so engulfed by the Holy Spirit as Jesus' life was. The presence of the Holy Spirit was evident in every phase of His life.

READING

Acts 10:38, *"How God anointed Jesus of Nazareth with the Holy Spirit and with power, who went about doing good and healing all who were oppressed by the devil, for God was with Him."*

1. PROPHECIES ABOUT CHRIST AND THE HOLY SPIRIT

A. Isaiah 11:2, *The Spirit of the LORD shall rest upon Him, the Spirit of wisdom and understanding, the Spirit of counsel and might, the Spirit of knowledge and of the fear of the LORD.*

B. Isaiah 61:1, *"The Spirit of the Lord GOD is upon Me, because the LORD has anointed Me to preach good tidings to the poor; He has sent Me to heal the brokenhearted, to proclaim liberty to the captives, and the opening of the prison to those who are bound."*

Christ confirmed this prophecy.

Luke 4:18, *"The Spirit of the LORD is upon Me, because He has anointed Me to preach the gospel to the poor; He has sent Me to heal the brokenhearted, to proclaim liberty to the captives and recovery of sight to the blind, to set at liberty those who are oppressed."*

2. CHRIST WAS BORN OF THE HOLY SPIRIT

Matthew 1:18, *Now the birth of Jesus Christ was as follows: After His mother Mary was betrothed to Joseph, before they came together, she was found with child of the Holy Spirit.*

3. CHRIST'S BAPTISM

The Holy Spirit witnessed Christ's baptism.

John 1:32, *And John bore witness, saying, "I saw the Spirit descending from heaven like a dove, and He remained upon Him."*

Matthew 3:13-17, *Then Jesus came from Galilee to John at the Jordan to be baptized by him.*

v. 14, *And John tried to prevent Him, saying, "I have need to be baptized by You, and are You coming to me?"*

v. 15, *But Jesus answered and said to him, "Permit it to be so now, for thus it is fitting for us to fulfill all righteousness." Then he allowed Him.*

v. 16, *Then Jesus, when He had been baptized, came up immediately from the water; and behold, the heavens were opened to Him, and He saw the Spirit of God descending like a dove and alighting upon Him.*

v. 17, *And suddenly a voice came from heaven, saying, "This is My beloved Son, in whom I am well pleased."*

The dove is the perfect emblem of the Holy Spirit to rest upon Christ.

4. DURING HIS TEMPTATION

The Holy Spirit witnessed Christ's temptation.

Mark 1:12-13, *And immediately the Spirit drove Him into the wilderness.*

v. 13, *And He was there in the wilderness forty days, tempted by Satan, and was with the wild beasts; and the angels ministered to Him.*

Luke 4:1, *Then Jesus, being filled with the Holy Spirit, returned from the Jordan and was led by the Spirit into the wilderness.*

Matthew 4:1, *Then Jesus was led up by the Spirit into the wilderness to be tempted by the devil.*

The Holy Spirit led Jesus into the wilderness.

5. CHRIST POSSESSED THE HOLY SPIRIT WITHOUT LIMIT

John 3:34, *For He whom God has sent speaks the words of God, for God does not give the Spirit by measure.*

6. CHRIST CAST OUT DEVILS BY THE HOLY SPIRIT

Matthew 12:28, *But if I cast out demons by the Spirit of God, surely the kingdom of God has come upon you.*

7. THE CRUCIFIXION OF JESUS CHRIST

The Holy Spirit witnessed the crucifixion.

Hebrews 9:14, *How much more shall the blood of Christ, who through the eternal Spirit offered Himself without spot to God, purge your conscience from dead works to serve the living God?*

8. THE HOLY SPIRIT WAS AT THE RESURRECTION

Romans 8:11, *But if the Spirit of Him who raised Jesus from the dead dwells in you, He who raised Christ from the dead will also give life to your mortal bodies through His Spirit who dwells in you.*

Romans 1:4, *And declared to be the Son of God with power according to the Spirit of holiness, by the resurrection from the dead.*

I Peter 3:18, *For Christ also suffered once for sins, the just for the unjust, that He might bring us to God, being put to death in the flesh but made alive by the Spirit.*

9. CHRIST'S ASCENSION

The witness of the Spirit can also be seen at the Ascension.

Acts 1:2, *Until the day in which He was taken up, after He through the Holy Spirit had given commandments to the apostles whom He had chosen.*

10. THE PARACLETE STATEMENTS

The Greek word, *parakletos* or *paraclete,* means "comforter."

A. The Holy Spirit reveals Christ.

John 16:14, *He will glorify Me, for He will take of what is Mine and declare it to you.*

B. The Holy Spirit is the Spirit of truth.

John 14:17, *"Even the Spirit of truth, whom the world cannot receive, because it neither sees Him nor knows Him; but you know Him, for He dwells with you and will be in you."*

C. The Holy Spirit is the Teacher.

John 14:26, *"But the Helper, the Holy Spirit, whom the Father will send in My name, He will teach you all things, and bring to your remembrance all things that I said to you."*

D. The Holy Spirit gives life.

John 6:63, *"It is the Spirit who gives life; the flesh profits nothing. The words that I speak to you are spirit, and they are life."*

E. The Holy Spirit testifies.

John 15:26-27, *"But when the Helper comes, whom I shall send to you from the Father, the Spirit of truth who proceeds from the Father, He will testify of Me.*

v. 27, *"And you also will bear witness, because you have been with Me from the beginning."*

F. The Holy Spirit is a guide who declares the things to come.

John 16:13, *"However, when He, the Spirit of truth, has come, He will guide you into all truth; for He will not speak on His own authority, but whatever He hears He will speak; and He will tell you things to come."*

NOTES

_____
_____
_____
_____
_____
_____
_____
_____
_____
_____
_____
_____
_____
_____
_____
_____
_____
_____
_____
_____
_____
_____
_____
_____
_____
_____
_____
_____
_____
_____
_____
_____
_____
_____

STUDY GUIDE

INDIANA CHRISTIAN UNIVERSITY

THE PERSON OF
THE HOLY SPIRIT

Lesson 11

THE WORK OF THE HOLY SPIRIT
IN THE EARLY CHURCH

INTRODUCTION

The operation of the Holy Spirit is not new in this dispensation. He has been operating throughout eternity.

READING

Romans 8:14, *For as many as are led by the Spirit of God, these are sons of God.*

1. IGNORANCE OF THE HOLY SPIRIT

Misconception and ignorance about the Holy Spirit and His work cause weakness and inefficiency.

2. THE HOLY SPIRIT IS RELATED TO PLANET EARTH

He created the earth by turning chaos into cosmos in Genesis 1.

3. THE WORK OF THE HOLY SPIRIT IS EVERLASTING

He was actively involved in the life of every Christian in the early Church.

4. THE HOLY SPIRIT HAS WORKED IN ALL DISPENSATIONS

He will continue working during the Great Tribulation.

5. THE INAUGURATION OF A NEW DISPENSATION

The dispensation which began at Pentecost is the dispensation of the Holy Spirit.

Acts 2:1-4, *Now when the Day of Pentecost had fully come, they were all with one accord in one place.*

v. 2, *And suddenly there came a sound from heaven, as of a rushing mighty wind, and it filled the whole house where they were sitting.*

v. 3, *Then there appeared to them divided tongues, as of fire, and one sat upon each of them.*

v. 4, *And they were all filled with the Holy Spirit and began to speak with other tongues, as the Spirit gave them utterance.*

The arrival of the Holy Spirit was announced by:

A. A voice from heaven

B. The sound of a mighty, rushing wind

C. Fire

D. Other tongues

E. The conversion of 3,000 people

6. THE HOLY SPIRIT AND THE NEW TESTAMENT DISCIPLES

A. Jesus told His disciples about the coming of the Holy Spirit.

John 14:16-17, *And I will pray the Father, and He will give you another Helper, that He may abide with you forever,*

v. 17, *Even the Spirit of truth, whom the world cannot receive, because it neither sees Him nor knows Him; but you know Him, for He dwells with you and will be in you.*

B. Romans 8:9, *But you are not in the flesh but in the Spirit, if indeed the Spirit of God dwells in you. Now if anyone does not have the Spirit of Christ, he is not His.*

The facts of promise became factors of power!

7. THE GIFT OF THE HOLY SPIRIT

A. The outpouring of the Holy Spirit was prophesied in the Old Testament.

Joel 2:28-29, *And it shall come to pass afterward that I will pour out My Spirit on all flesh; Your sons and your daughters shall prophesy, Your old men shall dream dreams, Your young men shall see visions.*

v. 29, *And also on My menservants and on My maidservants I will pour out My Spirit in those days.*

B. This promise was fulfilled on the day of Pentecost.

Acts 2:16, 33, *But this is what was spoken by the prophet Joel.*

v. 33, *Therefore being exalted to the right hand of God, and having received from the Father the promise of the Holy Spirit, He poured out this which you now see and hear.*

C. Jesus promised the Church the Holy Spirit would stay forever.

John 14:16, *And I will pray the Father, and He will give you another Helper, that He may abide with you forever.*

8. THE THREE-FOLD WORK OF THE HOLY SPIRIT

The Holy Spirit is a person. Jesus designated Him as "He" not as an "it." He is the Comforter, the Paraclete of God.

A. The Holy Spirit convicts men of sin. When people are dead to God, He convicts them.

   1) Conviction of sin comes from the Holy Spirit.

      John 16:7-11, *"Nevertheless I tell you the truth. It is to your advantage that I go away; for if I do not go away, the Helper will not come to you; but if I depart, I will send Him to you.*

      v. 8, *"And when He has come, He will convict the world of sin, and of righteousness, and of judgment:*

      v. 9, *"of sin, because they do not believe in Me;*

      v. 10, *"of righteousness, because I go to My Father and you see Me no more;*

      v. 11, *"of judgment, because the ruler of this world is judged."*

   2) The Holy Spirit convicts the world that Jesus, who is now ascended to heaven, is just as powerful in this present world as He was while He was on earth.

      Matthew 28:18, *Then Jesus came and spoke to them, saying, "All authority has been given to Me in heaven and on earth."*

   3) The Holy Spirit glorifies Jesus by proclaiming that He is Lord.

      John 16:13, *"However, when He, the Spirit of truth, has come, He will guide you into all truth; for He will not speak on His own authority, but whatever He hears He will speak; and He will tell you things to come."*

   4) The Holy Spirit confirms the believer's relationship with the Lord.

      I John 3:2, *Beloved, now we are children of God; and it has not yet been revealed what we shall be, but we know that when He is revealed, we shall be like Him, for we shall see Him as He is.*

5) When the Holy Spirit spoke through Peter at Pentecost, He convinced the audience of the righteousness of Jesus. Three thousand converts were the result of this anointed message.

C. The Holy Spirit convicts men in judgment.

Revelation 11:13, *In the same hour there was a great earthquake, and a tenth of the city fell. In the earthquake seven thousand people were killed, and the rest were afraid and gave glory to the God of heaven.*

1) The devil controls many of the world's systems today.

    a) An educational system which teaches there is no God

    b) Governments make laws against the Law of God

    c) The economy

    d) Religion

2) The Holy Spirit convinces men that these systems are under God's judgment.

3) The Holy Spirit reveals that we as Christians are more than conquerors through Christ over this world.

Romans 8:37, *Yet in all these things we are more than conquerors through Him who loved us.*

9. PETER RECEIVED A VISION FROM THE HOLY SPIRIT

Acts 10:19-20, *While Peter thought about the vision, the Spirit said to him, "Behold, three men are seeking you.*

v. 20, *"Arise therefore, go down and go with them, doubting nothing; for I have sent them."*

10. HOLY SPIRIT CHOSE PAUL AND BARNABAS

Acts 13:2, *As they ministered to the Lord and fasted, the Holy Spirit said, "Now separate to Me Barnabas and Saul for the work to which I have called them."*

11. HOLY SPIRIT FORBADE PAUL TO GO TO ASIA

Acts 16:6, *Now when they had gone through Phrygia and the region of Galatia, they were forbidden by the Holy Spirit to preach the word in Asia.*

12. THE SPIRIT GIVES LIFE

II Corinthians 3:6, *Who also made us sufficient as ministers of the new covenant, not of the letter but of the Spirit; for the letter kills, but the Spirit gives life.*

CONCLUSION

The truth of the Person of the Holy Spirit was nearly lost during the Dark, or Middle Ages.

The closer the Church is to the return of Christ, the more powerful the influence of the Holy Spirit becomes. Those who do not believe in the second coming of Christ know very little about the Person of the Holy Spirit.

STUDY GUIDE

INDIANA CHRISTIAN UNIVERSITY

THE PERSON OF
THE HOLY SPIRIT

Lesson 12

THE DEMANDS OF THE PERSON
OF THE HOLY SPIRIT

INTRODUCTION

The requirements God the Father has for human beings is often taught.

The demands of the Lord Jesus upon His disciples are loudly proclaimed.

The authority of the Third Person of the Trinity over believers is seldom mentioned. When we seek the Holy Spirit, the knowledge of the mind of the Spirit becomes easily available.

READING

Romans 8:27, *Now He who searches the hearts knows what the mind of the Spirit is, because He makes intercession for the saints according to the will of God.*

Isaiah 4:4, *When the Lord has washed away the filth of the daughters of Zion, and purged the blood of Jerusalem from her midst, by the spirit of judgment and by the spirit of burning. . .*

1. THE HOLY SPIRIT WARNS ABOUT DEMON ACTIVITY

I Timothy 4:1, *Now the Spirit expressly says that in latter times some will depart from the faith, giving heed to deceiving spirits and doctrines of demons.*

Galatians 5:16-17, *I say then: Walk in the Spirit, and you shall not fulfill the lust of the flesh.*

v. 17, *For the flesh lusts against the Spirit, and the Spirit against the flesh; and these are contrary to one another, so that you do not do the things that you wish.*

2. THE HOLY SPIRIT DEMANDS CONTROL OVER THE HUMAN MIND

Philippians 2:5, *Let this mind be in you which was also in Christ Jesus.*

I Corinthians 2:16, *For "who has known the mind of the LORD that he may instruct Him?" But we have the mind of Christ.*

3. THE HOLY SPIRIT HAS THE FINAL WORD IN TEACHING AND ADMINISTRATION

John 16:13, *"However, when He, the Spirit of truth, has come, He will guide you into all truth; for He will not speak on His own authority, but whatever He hears He will speak; and He will tell you things to come."*

Galatians 5:18, 25, *But if you are led by the Spirit, you are not under the law.*

v. 25, *If we live in the Spirit, let us also walk in the Spirit.*

4. THE HOLY SPIRIT DEMANDS WE NOT BE IGNORANT

I Corinthians 12:1, *Now concerning spiritual gifts, brethren, I do not want you to be ignorant.*

I Peter 2:15, *For this is the will of God, that by doing good you may put to silence the ignorance of foolish men.*

II Peter 3:8, *But, beloved, do not forget this one thing, that with the Lord one day is as a thousand years, and a thousand years as one day.*

5. THE HOLY SPIRIT DEMANDS FRUITFULNESS IN CHRISTIAN LIVES

Galatians 5:22-25, *But the fruit of the Spirit is love, joy, peace, long-suffering, kindness, goodness, faithfulness,*

v. 23, *gentleness, self-control. Against such there is no law.*

v. 24, *And those who are Christ's have crucified the flesh with its passions and desires.*

v. 25, *If we live in the Spirit, let us also walk in the Spirit.*

A. The first three fruit are dedicated to God–love, joy, and peace.

B. The second three are dedicated to our fellowman–longsuffering, gentleness, and goodness.

C. The third three are directed toward oneself–faith, meekness, and temperance.

6. THE HOLY SPIRIT DEMANDS UNITY

Philippians 1:27, *Only let your conduct be worthy of the gospel of Christ, so that whether I come and see you or am absent, I may hear of your affairs, that you stand fast in one spirit, with one mind striving together for the faith of the gospel.*

I Corinthians 12:12-13, *For as the body is one and has many members, but all the members of that one body, being many, are one body, so also is Christ.*

v. 13, *For by one Spirit we were all baptized into one body—whether Jews or Greeks, whether slaves or free—and have all been made to drink into one Spirit.*

NOTES

THE PERSON OF
THE HOLY SPIRIT

Lesson 13

THE SIN AGAINST
THE PERSON OF THE HOLY SPIRIT

INTRODUCTION

Man's greatest questions concern the sin against the Holy Spirit. The Holy Spirit can be blasphemed. This blasphemy is the unpardonable sin.

Blasphemy means "to make an affront to God by acts, signs, writings or words."

Blasphemy can also mean "to commit an act of claiming to be deity."

Blasphemy is defamatory like cursing or reviling God. It is the strongest intentional, volitional indignity against God.

Mankind can commit many wrongs and break many divine laws, but the Holy Spirit judges the world. There has to be a stopping place. The sin against the Holy Spirit is the ultimate, unforgivable sin.

John 16:8, *"And when He has come, He will convict the world of sin, and of righteousness, and of judgment."*

READING

Matthew 12:31, *"Therefore I say to you, every sin and blasphemy will be forgiven men, but the blasphemy against the Spirit will not be forgiven men."*

Mark 3:28-29, *"Assuredly, I say to you, all sins will be forgiven the sons of men, and whatever blasphemies they may utter;*

v. 29, *"but he who blasphemes against the Holy Spirit never has forgiveness, but is subject to eternal condemnation."*

Matthew 15:19, *"For out of the heart proceed evil thoughts, murders, adulteries, fornications, thefts, false witness, blasphemies."*

1. WHO DOES NOT COMMIT THE SIN AGAINST THE HOLY SPIRIT?

The backslider has not committed the unpardonable sin. God wants to bring the backslider to repentance.

2. WHAT IS BLASPHEMY AGAINST THE HOLY SPIRIT?

In order to blaspheme the Holy Spirit one must:

A. Hate and despise the Spirit.

B. Hate Jesus Christ who sent the Spirit.

C. Hate God the Father who sent the Spirit.

D. Hate the Church, birthed by Jesus Christ through the Holy Spirit.

E. Hate the Bible which is the voice of God through Jesus Christ and the Holy Spirit.

3. JESUS CHRIST WAS ACCUSED OF BLASPHEMY

Matthew 9:3, *And at once some of the scribes said within themselves, "This Man blasphemes!"*

Matthew 26:65, *Then the high priest tore his clothes, saying, "He has spoken blasphemy! What further need do we have of witnesses? Look, now you have heard His blasphemy!*

John 10:33, *The Jews answered Him, saying, "For a good work we do not stone You, but for blasphemy, and because You, being a Man, make Yourself God."*

4. CURSING THE HOLY SPIRIT

A. When you curse the postman because he delivers the mail, you actually curse the person who sent it. Jesus sent the Holy Spirit, so if you curse the Holy Spirit you actually curse Jesus Christ.

B. Jesus came in the Father's name, so to curse Christ is the same as cursing God the Father.

NOTES

_____

_____

_____

_____

_____

_____

_____

_____

_____

_____

_____

_____

_____

_____

_____

_____

_____

_____

_____

_____

_____

_____

_____

_____

_____

_____

_____

_____

STUDY GUIDE

INDIANA CHRISTIAN UNIVERSITY

THE PERSON OF
THE HOLY SPIRIT

Lesson 14

THE HOLY SPIRIT INTERCEDES

INTRODUCTION

Intercession is a potent reality of the Holy Spirit. Intercession is prayer and entreaty to God on behalf of another. Its purpose is to fulfill a need and effect reconciliation.

READING

Romans 8:26-27, *Likewise the Spirit also helps in our weaknesses. For we do not know what we should pray for as we ought, but the Spirit Himself makes intercession for us with groanings which cannot be uttered.*

v. 27, *Now He who searches the hearts knows what the mind of the Spirit is, because He makes intercession for the saints according to the will of God.*

1. INTERCESSION IS AN ACTION OF THE SPIRIT

It is not soulical or physical, but spiritual.

2. MOSES KNEW INTERCESSION THROUGH HIS SPIRIT

Exodus 32:31-32, *Then Moses returned to the LORD and said, "Oh, these people have sinned a great sin, and have made for themselves a god of gold!*

v. 32, *"Yet now, if You will forgive their sin—but if not, I pray, blot me out of Your book which You have written."*

84

3. GOD SEEKS INTERCESSORS

Isaiah 59:16, *He saw that there was no man, and wondered that there was no intercessor; Therefore His own arm brought salvation for Him; And His own righteousness, it sustained Him.*

4. CHRIST HAS ALWAYS BEEN INVOLVED WITH INTERCESSION

A. Hebrews 2:17, *Therefore, in all things He had to be made like His brethren, that He might be a merciful and faithful High Priest in things pertaining to God, to make propitiation for the sins of the people.*

B. Jesus interceded for those who killed Him.

Luke 23:34, *Then Jesus said, "Father, forgive them, for they do not know what they do." And they divided His garments and cast lots.*

C. Jesus interceded for Peter.

Luke 22:31-32, *And the Lord said, "Simon, Simon! Indeed, Satan has asked for you, that he may sift you as wheat.*

v. 32, *"But I have prayed for you, that your faith should not fail; and when you have returned to Me, strengthen your brethren."*

D. Christ intercedes for us even now.

Romans 8:34, *Who is he who condemns? It is Christ who died, and furthermore is also risen, who is even at the right hand of God, who also makes intercession for us.*

Hebrews 7:25, *Therefore He is also able to save to the uttermost those who come to God through Him, since He always lives to make intercession for them.*

5. PAUL REQUESTED INTERCESSION

Romans 15:30, *Now I beg you, brethren, through the Lord Jesus Christ, and through the love of the Spirit, that you strive together with me in prayers to God for me.*

6. THE HOLY SPIRIT MAKES INTERCESSION

Romans 8:26, *Likewise the Spirit also helps in our weaknesses. For we do not know what we should pray for as we ought, but the Spirit Himself makes intercession for us with groanings which cannot be uttered.*

NOTES

_____

_____

_____

_____

_____

_____

_____

_____

_____

_____

_____

_____

_____

_____

_____

_____

_____

_____

_____

_____

_____

_____

_____

_____

_____

_____

_____

_____

_____

_____

THE PERSON OF
THE HOLY SPIRIT

Lesson 15

THE HOLY SPIRIT IMPARTS POWER

INTRODUCTION

The Holy Spirit operates in power. On the first page of the Bible, the Holy Spirit functioned in creation.

Genesis 1:2, *The earth was without form, and void; and darkness was on the face of the deep. And the Spirit of God was hovering over the face of the waters.*

The Holy Spirit began His dispensation with prayer from Jesus Christ.

John 14:16, *"And I will pray the Father, and He will give you another Helper, that He may abide with you forever."*

The final page of the Scriptures closes with His energetic plea to the Church.

Revelation 22:17, *And the Spirit and the bride say, "Come!" And let him who hears say, "Come!" And let him who thirsts come. Whoever desires, let him take the water of life freely.*

READING

Acts 1:8, *"But you shall receive power when the Holy Spirit has come upon you; and you shall be witnesses to Me in Jerusalem, and in all Judea and Samaria, and to the end of the earth."*

1. SAMSON

Samson's mighty acts occurred through the Holy Spirit.

A. He killed a lion with the Holy Spirit's power.

Judges 14:5-6, *So Samson went down to Timnah with his father and mother, and came to the vineyards of Timnah. Now to his surprise, a young lion came roaring against him.*

v. 6, *And the Spirit of the LORD came mightily upon him, and he tore the lion apart as one would have torn apart a young goat, though he had nothing in his hand. But he did not tell his father or his mother what he had done.*

B. He slew thirty men by the Holy Spirit's power.

Judges 14:19, *Then the Spirit of the LORD came upon him mightily, and he went down to Ashkelon and killed thirty of their men, took their apparel, and gave the changes of clothing to those who had explained the riddle. So his anger was aroused, and he went back up to his father's house.*

C. He slew 1,000 men with the Holy Spirit's power.

Judges 15:14-15, *When he came to Lehi, the Philistines came shouting against him. Then the Spirit of the LORD came mightily upon him; and the ropes that were on his arms became like flax that is burned with fire, and his bonds broke loose from his hands.*

v. 15, *He found a fresh jawbone of a donkey, reached out his hand and took it, and killed a thousand men with it.*

2. SAUL

King Saul knew the power of the Holy Spirit.

I Samuel 11:6-7, *Then the Spirit of God came upon Saul when he heard this news, and his anger was greatly aroused.*

v. 7, *So he took a yoke of oxen and cut them in pieces, and sent them throughout all the territory of Israel by the hands of messengers, saying, "Whoever does not go out with Saul and Samuel to battle, so it shall be done to his oxen." And the fear of the LORD fell on the people, and they came out with one consent.*

3. DAVID

David was anointed with the Spirit.

I Samuel 16:13, *Then Samuel took the horn of oil and anointed him in the midst of his brothers; and the Spirit of the LORD came upon David from that day forward. So Samuel arose and went to Ramah.*

4. ELIJAH AND ELISHA

Elijah and Elisha knew the power of the Holy Spirit.

II Kings 2:9, *And so it was, when they had crossed over, that Elijah said to Elisha, "Ask! What may I do for you, before I am taken away from you?" Elisha said, "Please let a double portion of your spirit be upon me."*

5. ISAIAH

Isaiah prophesied about the power of the Holy Spirit.

A. Isaiah 11:2, *The Spirit of the LORD shall rest upon Him, the Spirit of wisdom and understanding, the Spirit of counsel and might, the Spirit of knowledge and of the fear of the LORD.*

B. Isaiah 61:1-3, *"The Spirit of the Lord GOD is upon Me, because the LORD has anointed Me to preach good tidings to the poor; He has sent Me to heal the brokenhearted, to proclaim liberty to the captives, and the opening of the prison to those who are bound;*

v. 2, *To proclaim the acceptable year of the LORD, and the day of vengeance of our God; To comfort all who mourn,*

v. 3, *To console those who mourn in Zion, to give them beauty for ashes, the oil of joy for mourning, the garment of praise for the spirit of heaviness; That they may be called trees of righteousness, the planting of the LORD, that He may be glorified."*

6. JOEL

Joel prophesied about the outpouring of the Holy Spirit.

Joel 2:28-29, *"And it shall come to pass afterward that I will pour out My Spirit on all flesh; Your sons and your daughters shall prophesy, your old men shall dream dreams, your young men shall see visions;*

v. 29, *And also on My menservants and on My maidservants I will pour out My Spirit in those days."*

7. MICAH

Micah knew the might of the Spirit.

Micah 3:8, *But truly I am full of power by the Spirit of the LORD, and of justice and might, to declare to Jacob his transgression and to Israel his sin.*

8. JESUS

Jesus ministered in the power of the Holy Spirit.

A. Matthew 12:28, *"But if I cast out demons by the Spirit of God, surely the kingdom of God has come upon you."*

B. Luke 4:14, *Then Jesus returned in the power of the Spirit to Galilee, and news of Him went out through all the surrounding region.*

C. Luke 4:18-19, *"The Spirit of the LORD is upon Me, because He has anointed Me to preach the gospel to the poor. He has sent Me to heal the brokenhearted, to preach deliverance to the captives and recovery of sight to the blind, to set at liberty those who are oppressed,*

v. 19, *To preach the acceptable year of the LORD."*

D. John 6:63, *"It is the Spirit who gives life; the flesh profits nothing. The words that I speak to you are spirit, and they are life."*

E. Acts 10:38, *"How God anointed Jesus of Nazareth with the Holy Spirit and with power, who went about doing good and healing all who were oppressed by the devil, for God was with Him."*

9. THE DISCIPLES OF JESUS

Jesus promised the power of the Holy Spirit to His disciples.

A. Mark 13:11, *"But when they arrest you and deliver you up, do not worry beforehand, or premeditate what you will speak. But whatever is given you in that hour, speak that; for it is not you who speak, but the Holy Spirit."*

B. Luke 24:49, *"Behold, I send the Promise of My Father upon you; but tarry in the city of Jerusalem until you are endued with power from on high."*

C. Acts 1:8, *"But you shall receive power when the Holy Spirit has come upon you; and you shall be witnesses to Me in Jerusalem, and in all Judea and Samaria, and to the end of the earth."*

10. THE EARLY CHURCH

The early Church was empowered by the Spirit.

A. They were baptized in the Spirit and given a new language.

Acts 2:4, *And they were all filled with the Holy Spirit and began to speak with other tongues, as the Spirit gave them utterance.*

Acts 2:38, *Then Peter said to them, "Repent, and let every one of you be baptized in the name of Jesus Christ for the remission of sins; and you shall receive the gift of the Holy Spirit."*

B. They were filled with boldness.

Acts 4:31, *And when they had prayed, the place where they were assembled together was shaken; and they were all filled with the Holy Spirit, and they spoke the word of God with boldness.*

C. They performed wonders and miracles in Jesus' name.

Acts 6:8, *And Stephen, full of faith and power, did great wonders and signs among the people.*

Hebrews 2:4, *God also bearing witness both with signs and wonders, with various miracles, and gifts of the Holy Spirit, according to His own will?*

D. They prophesied.

Acts 19:6, *And when Paul had laid hands on them, the Holy Spirit came upon them, and they spoke with tongues and prophesied.*

E. They were sealed by the Holy Spirit.

II Corinthians 1:21, *Now He who establishes us with you in Christ and has anointed us is God.*

11. PAUL

The Apostle Paul ministered in the power of the Spirit.

A. Acts 13:9-12, *Then Saul, who also is called Paul, filled with the Holy Spirit, looked intently at him*

v. 10, *and said, "O full of all deceit and all fraud, you son of the devil, you enemy of all righteousness, will you not cease perverting the straight ways of the Lord?*

v. 11, *"And now, indeed, the hand of the Lord is upon you, and you shall be blind, not seeing the sun for a time." And immediately a dark mist fell on him, and he went around seeking someone to lead him by the hand.*

v. 12, *Then the proconsul believed, when he saw what had been done, being astonished at the teaching of the Lord.*

B. Romans 15:19, *In mighty signs and wonders, by the power of the Spirit of God, so that from Jerusalem and round about to Illyricum I have fully preached the gospel of Christ.*

C. I Corinthians 2:4, *And my speech and my preaching were not with persuasive words of human wisdom, but in demonstration of the Spirit and of power.*

D. I Thessalonians 1:5, *For our gospel did not come to you in word only, but also in power, and in the Holy Spirit and in much assurance, as you know what kind of men we were among you for your sake.*

12. HOW TO RECEIVE THE POWER OF THE HOLY SPIRIT

A. Without fear

II Timothy 1:7, *For God has not given us a spirit of fear, but of power and of love and of a sound mind.*

B. By faith

Galatians 3:5, *Therefore He who supplies the Spirit to you and works miracles among you, does He do it by the works of the law, or by the hearing of faith?*

C. Through prayer

Jude 1:20, *But you, beloved, building yourselves up on your most holy faith, praying in the Holy Spirit. . .*

D. Through the gifts of the Spirit

I Corinthians 12:8-11, *For to one is given the word of wisdom through the Spirit, to another the word of knowledge through the same Spirit,*

v. 9, *to another faith by the same Spirit, to another gifts of healings by the same Spirit,*

v. 10, *to another the working of miracles, to another prophecy, to another discerning of spirits, to another different kinds of tongues, to another the interpretation of tongues.*

v. 11, *But one and the same Spirit works all these things, distributing to each one individually as He wills.*

E. Through love

I Corinthians 13:1-3, *Though I speak with the tongues of men and of angels, but have not love, I have become sounding brass or a clanging cymbal.*

v. 2, *And though I have the gift of prophecy, and understand all mysteries and all knowledge, and though I have all faith, so that I could remove mountains, but have not love, I am nothing.*

v. 3, *And though I bestow all my goods to feed the poor, and though I give my body to be burned, but have not love, it profits me nothing.*

F. In your mortal body

Romans 8:11, *But if the Spirit of Him who raised Jesus from the dead dwells in you, He who raised Christ from the dead will also give life to your mortal bodies through His Spirit who dwells in you.*

13. THE WORK OF THE HOLY SPIRIT IN MAN

A. A human being can be born of the Spirit.

John 3:5-6, *Jesus answered, "Most assuredly, I say to you, unless one is born of water and the Spirit, he cannot enter the kingdom of God.*

v. 6, *"That which is born of the flesh is flesh, and that which is born of the Spirit is spirit."*

Galatians 4:29, *But, as he who was born according to the flesh then persecuted him who was born according to the Spirit, even so it is now.*

B. The Holy Spirit brings sanctification.

I Peter 1:2, *Elect according to the foreknowledge of God the Father, in sanctification of the Spirit, for obedience and sprinkling of the blood of Jesus Christ: Grace to you and peace be multiplied.*

II Thessalonians 2:13, *But we are bound to give thanks to God always for you, brethren beloved by the Lord, because God from the beginning chose you for salvation through sanctification by the Spirit and belief in the truth.*

C. He leads to holiness.

Romans 1:4, *And declared to be the Son of God with power, according to the Spirit of holiness, by the resurrection from the dead.*

D. The Holy Spirit guides.

Romans 8:14, *For as many as are led by the Spirit of God, these are sons of God.*

E. The Holy Spirit anoints.

14. THE HOLY SPIRIT IS MAN'S SOURCE OF HOPE

A. Galatians 5:5, *For we through the Spirit eagerly wait for the hope of righteousness by faith.*

B. Romans 8:11, *But if the Spirit of Him who raised Jesus from the dead dwells in you, He who raised Christ from the dead will also give life to your mortal bodies through His Spirit who dwells in you.*

15. THE HOLY SPIRIT FIGHTS THE ENEMY

The Holy Spirit shields us from our enemies.

Isaiah 59:19, *So shall they fear the name of the LORD from the west, and His glory from the rising of the sun; When the enemy comes in like a flood, the Spirit of the LORD will lift up a standard against him.*

INDIANA CHRISTIAN UNIVERSITY

THE PERSON OF
THE HOLY SPIRIT

Lesson 16

THE HOLY SPIRIT REVEALS THE FUTURE

INTRODUCTION

Jesus said the Holy Spirit would tell us what He hears from the Father. These messages from the Spirit include revelations of future events.

READING

John 16:13, *"However, when He, the Spirit of truth, has come, He will guide you into all truth; for He will not speak on His own authority, but whatever He hears He will speak; and He will tell you things to come."*

1. PHARAOH'S DREAMS

The Holy Spirit revealed the coming drought in Egypt to Joseph through Pharaoh's dreams.

Genesis 41:25, 29-30, 38, *Then Joseph said to Pharaoh, "The dreams of Pharaoh are one; God has shown Pharaoh what He is about to do.*

v. 29, *"Indeed seven years of great plenty will come throughout all the land of Egypt;*

v. 30, *"but after them seven years of famine will arise, and all the plenty will be forgotten in the land of Egypt; and the famine will deplete the land."*

v. 38, *And Pharaoh said to his servants, "Can we find such a one as this, a man in whom is the Spirit of God?"*

2. THE WRITING ON THE WALL

The Holy Spirit revealed the future through Daniel's interpretation of the writing on the wall. That same night Babylon fell to the Persians and Medes.

Daniel 5:12, *"Inasmuch as an excellent spirit, knowledge, understanding, interpreting dreams, solving riddles, and explaining enigmas were found in this Daniel, whom the king named Belteshazzar, now let Daniel be called, and he will give the interpretation."*

3. THE PROPHETS

Ezekiel prophesied by the Holy Spirit.

Ezekiel 11:5, *Then the Spirit of the LORD fell upon me, and said to me, "Speak! 'Thus says the LORD: "Thus you have said, O house of Israel; for I know the things that come into your mind."*

4. THE COMPANY OF THE PROPHETS

King Saul prophesied under the power of the Holy Spirit when he was in the company of prophets.

I Samuel 10:10, *When they came there to the hill, there was a group of prophets to meet him; then the Spirit of God came upon him, and he prophesied among them.*

5. THE WORD ON HIS TONGUE

King David spoke through the power of the Spirit of the Lord.

II Samuel 23:1-2, *Now these are the last words of David. Thus says David the son of Jesse; Thus says the man raised up on high, the anointed of the God of Jacob, and the sweet psalmist of Israel:*

v. 2, *"The Spirit of the LORD spoke by me, and His word was on my tongue."*

6. GOD WANTS TO USE EVERYONE

The revelation of the future is open to all: young and old, male and female.

Joel 2:28-29, *"And it shall come to pass afterward that I will pour out My Spirit on all flesh; Your sons and your daughters shall prophesy, your old men shall dream dreams, your young men shall see visions;*

v. 29, *And also on My menservants and on My maidservants I will pour out My Spirit in those days."*

7. THE SPIRIT OF PROPHECY

The testimony of Jesus is the spirit of prophecy.

Revelation 19:10, *And I fell at his feet to worship him. But he said to me, "See that you do not do that! I am your fellow servant, and of your brethren who have the testimony of Jesus. Worship God! For the testimony of Jesus is the spirit of prophecy."*

8. THE REVELATION OF THE SPIRIT

A. He gives pertinent knowledge to the Church.

Revelation 2:7, *"He who has an ear, let him hear what the Spirit says to the churches. To him who overcomes I will give to eat from the tree of life, which is in the midst of the Paradise of God."*

B. Paul knew his future through the Spirit.

Acts 20:22-23, *"And see, now I go bound in the spirit to Jerusalem, not knowing the things that will happen to me there,*

v. 23, *"except that the Holy Spirit testifies in every city, saying that chains and tribulations await me."*

Acts 21:4, 11, *And finding disciples, we stayed there seven days. They told Paul through the Spirit not to go up to Jerusalem.*

v. 11, *When he had come to us, he took Paul's belt, bound his own hands and feet, and said, "Thus says the Holy Spirit, 'So shall the Jews at Jerusalem bind the man who owns this belt, and deliver him into the hands of the Gentiles.' "*

C. The Spirit revealed a coming famine.

Acts 11:27-28, *And in these days prophets came from Jerusalem to Antioch.*

v. 28, *Then one of them, named Agabus, stood up and showed by the Spirit that there was going to be a great famine throughout all the world, which also happened in the days of Claudius Caesar.*

D. The conditions of the end times are foretold by the Spirit.

I Timothy 4:1-3, *Now the Spirit expressly says that in latter times some will depart from the faith, giving heed to deceiving spirits and doctrines of demons,*

v. 2, *speaking lies in hypocrisy, having their own conscience seared with a hot iron,*

v. 3, *forbidding to marry, and commanding to abstain from foods which God created to be received with thanksgiving by those who believe and know the truth.*

9. THE WORD OF WISDOM

The Holy Spirit reveals the future through the gift of the word of wisdom.

A. The gift of the word of wisdom is not a person's brilliance or academic success in a given subject. The gift has nothing to do with worldly wisdom.

B. The gift of the word of wisdom is a supernatural revelation of the divine purposes of God in Christ, communicated by the Holy Spirit to the Church through a believer. This gift unveils, in part, the purposes of God on the earth.

I Corinthians 2:7, *But we speak the wisdom of God in a mystery, the hidden wisdom which God ordained before the ages for our glory.*

C. It is a fragment of God's wisdom.

1) The name of this gift is *the word of wisdom*. It is a fragment of the total wisdom of God, as a word is a fragment of a sentence. We receive a fragment of His wisdom. This means the word of wisdom is a portion of the great omniscience of God.

2) God knows the total future. When He conveys to the Church something He is going to do, He has made His servant wise in that one matter. That person may not be wise concerning other things. God alone is all-wise.

D. A personal function of the word of wisdom.

A number of years ago, in a simple wooden building in Tennessee, God revealed to me in a vision, a call to minister to the entire world. I saw millions of people marching past me into eternity.

At the same time in London, England, God communicated a message to Rev. Howard Carter saying that he must travel the world and minister. God told him that He had prepared a companion for him who lived in a distant place. He would be a stranger when he came and would make himself known by saying certain words. Rev. Carter was so impressed with this message from God that he wrote it down and disclosed it to his teaching staff and students in his Bible school in London.

Less than three years later, not knowing that God had spoken to Rev. Carter, I approached him at a campmeeting in Eureka Springs, Arkansas. God completely fulfilled the prophecy spoken to him in London England. In his hotel room, Howard Carter, Stanley Fordsham and I lifted up our hearts and thanked God that He could speak in these days. That moment began a most remarkable friendship. An Englishman and an American traveled throughout the world to minister and bless multitudes of people.

E. The word of wisdom and gift of prophecy.

A clear distinction must be formed regarding the simple inspirational gift of prophecy in the New Testament and the word of wisdom. I Corinthians 14:3 gives the full measure of the blessings of prophecy. There is no revelation associated with it. Any person speaking in the Church, foretelling the future, has left the simple and least of the gifts and has moved into the greatest and foremost of them. The prophet in the Old or New Testament is a seer, who sees the future and possesses the gift of the word of God's wisdom.

10. COVET THE GIFTS

Most cults are born because the Church does not utilize the gifts of God. For example, if the Church had prayed for the sick, Christian Science would not have a place in the world. If the Church had moved into the spiritual gifts of revelation (the word of wisdom, the word of knowledge and the discerning of spirits), there would be no need for fortunetellers, palm readers, crystal-ball gazers, Ouiji boards and all the other paraphernalia which the devil uses to deceive people.

We are engulfed in the greatest wave of black magic and witchcraft the world has ever known. One reason is that the Church does not operate in the gifts of the Spirit, that are its weapons of warfare. If they were in operation, the devil's counterfeits would stop completely. I challenge you to seek God for these major gifts of the Holy Spirit *But earnestly desire the best gifts* ...(I Corinthians 12:31), ...*desire spiritual gifts...* (I Corinthians 14:1).

STUDY GUIDE

INDIANA CHRISTIAN UNIVERSITY

THE PERSON OF
THE HOLY SPIRIT

Lesson 17

THE HOLY SPIRIT BESTOWS
GIFTS ON THE CHURCH

INTRODUCTION

One of the attributes of the Person of the Holy Spirit is the capability to bestow divine and spiritual gifts upon the Church. These mighty enablements are free. They are gifts. They become more abundant through operation of faith. There are nine gifts of the Holy Spirit which can be divided into three categories.

I Corinthians 12:11, *But one and the same Spirit works all these things, distributing to each one individually as He wills.*

READING

I Corinthians 12:1, 8-10, *Now concerning spiritual gifts, brethren, I do not want you to be ignorant. . .*

v. 8, *for to one is given the word of wisdom through the Spirit, to another the word of knowledge through the same Spirit,*

v. 9, *to another faith by the same Spirit, to another gifts of healings by the same Spirit,*

v. 10, *to another the working of miracles, to another prophecy, to another discerning of spirits, to another different kinds of tongues, to another the interpretation of tongues.*

II Corinthians 3:7-8, *But if the ministry of death, written and engraved on stones, was glorious, so that the children of Israel could not look steadily at the face of Moses because of the glory of his countenance, which glory was passing away,*

v. 8, *how will the ministry of the Spirit not be more glorious?*

1. THE GIFTS OF REVELATION

In the gifts of revelation, God reveals something from heaven to man. This revelation is something man cannot know any other way.

Matthew 16:17, *Jesus answered and said to him, "Blessed are you, Simon Bar-Jonah, for flesh and blood has not revealed this to you, but My Father who is in heaven."*

A. The word of wisdom reveals the prophetic future under God's anointing.

I Corinthians 2:7, *But we speak the wisdom of God in a mystery, the hidden wisdom which God ordained before the ages for our glory.*

B. The word of knowledge is the revelation of a fact currently in existence. This fact cannot be seen or heard naturally. It is knowledge supernaturally revealed by God.

C. The discerning of spirits has to do with the comprehension of the human spirit as supernaturally revealed by the Holy Spirit.

Acts 13:9-10, *Then Saul, who also is called Paul, filled with the Holy Spirit, looked intently at him*

v. 10, *and said, "O full of all deceit and all fraud, you son of the devil, you enemy of all righteousness, will you not cease perverting the straight ways of the Lord?"*

2. THE GIFTS OF POWER

A. The working of miracles occurs when, through the human instruments of hands, eyes, mouth or feet, a person supernaturally does something by the divine energy of the Holy Spirit. An example occurred when Samson killed a lion with his bare hands.

Judges 14:6, *And the Spirit of the LORD came mightily upon him, and he tore the lion apart as one would have torn apart a young goat, though he had nothing in his hand. But he did not tell his father or his mother what he had done.*

B. The gift of faith occurs when God brings a supernatural thing to pass without any human effort.

Matthew 21:19, *And seeing a fig tree by the road, He came to it and found nothing on it but leaves, and said to it, "Let no fruit grow on you ever again." Immediately the fig tree withered away.*

C. The gifts of healing occur when God supernaturally heals the sick. This is the only plural gift.

How many gifts of healing are there? It is possible that there are as many categories of disease as there were stripes upon the back of Jesus. This may mean that 39 different areas of sickness, such as congenital and organic ailments, sicknesses caused by neglect of the body, viruses, etc. However many categories there are ...*with His stripes we are healed* (Isaiah 53:5).

3. THE GIFTS OF INSPIRATION

A. The gift of prophecy occurs when an anointed person speaks words of edification, exhortation or comfort to the Church. This speech comes supernaturally without human forethought. This gift from God is to be regulated. No more than three prophecies are allowed in a single meeting.

I Corinthians 14:29, *Let two or three prophets speak, and let the others judge.*

B. The gift of speaking in tongues is the ministry of publicly proclaiming a message from God which is not understood by the person giving it.

I Corinthians 14:22, *Therefore tongues are for a sign, not to those who believe but to unbelievers; but prophesying is not for unbelievers but for those who believe.*

C. The gift of the interpretation of tongues occurs when a message given in another language is interpreted supernaturally by the Spirit. This interpretation does not actively involve the human mental facilities.

I Corinthians 14:4, *He who speaks in a tongue edifies himself, but he who prophesies edifies the church.*

4. THESE GIFTS ARE TO BE USED TODAY

We are living near the end of the last days.

Acts 2:17-18, *" 'And it shall come to pass in the last days, says God, that I will pour out of My Spirit on all flesh; your sons and your daughters shall prophesy, your young men shall see visions, your old men shall dream dreams.*

v. 18, *" 'And on My menservants and on My maidservants I will pour out My Spirit in those days; and they shall prophesy.' "*

THE PERSON OF
THE HOLY SPIRIT

Lesson 18

THE HOLY SPIRIT BEARS FRUIT

INTRODUCTION

It is interesting to note that the word "fruit" in Galatians chapter five is used in its singular, not plural form.

This distinction does not mean that there is only one fruit, or that it is impossible to distinguish between the attributes listed. The emphasis is that these various characteristics are from an identical source.

When the Scriptures speak of the fruit of the Spirit, all characteristics must function in order for an individual one to have validity. Love is not genuine love unless longsuffering is involved; therefore, these are not fruits which can be picked and chosen as in a supermarket. These qualities are the fruit of the Spirit!

The quality of any fruit depends on the quality and nature of the plant which produces it.

James 3:12, *Can a fig tree, my brethren, bear olives, or a grapevine bear figs? Thus no spring yields both salt water and fresh.*

READING

Galatians 5:22-23, *But the fruit of the Spirit is love, joy, peace, longsuffering, kindness, goodness, faithfulness,*

v. 23, *gentleness, self-control. Against such there is no law.*

1. A PLANT PRODUCES AFTER ITS OWN KIND

A plant of a certain species will naturally produce that type of fruit. If the Holy Spirit dwells within us, we should naturally produce the fruit of the Spirit. This does not mean we cannot help to cultivate that fruit. We can be sure we get the proper nourishment.

A. A plant needs good soil. We need to be rooted in love.

Ephesians 3:17, *That Christ may dwell in your hearts through faith; that you, being rooted and grounded in love. . .*

B. A plant needs plenty of water. We need the water of salvation.

Isaiah 12:3, *Therefore with joy you will draw water from the wells of salvation.*

C. A plant needs sunlight. We need to bask in the light of the Son, our Lord Jesus Christ.

Isaiah 60:19, *"The sun shall no longer be your light by day, nor for brightness shall the moon give light to you; but the LORD will be to you an everlasting light, and your God your glory."*

D. Modern horticulturists teach that we must speak to plants in order for them to thrive. Likewise, we must speak in the Spirit so that we may grow and thrive spiritually.

Ephesians 5:18-19, *And do not be drunk with wine, in which is dissipation; but be filled with the Spirit,*

v. 19, *speaking to one another in psalms and hymns and spiritual songs, singing and making melody in your heart to the Lord.*

E. A plant needs to be cared for by a gardener. We need our heavenly Husbandman.

John 15:2, *"Every branch in Me that does not bear fruit He takes away; and every branch that bears fruit He prunes, that it may bear more fruit."*

2. THE FRUIT OF THE SPIRIT

The character of God is the basis for the fruit of the Spirit.

A. II Corinthians 13:11 teaches about the God of love and peace.

B. I John 4:8 plainly declares God is love.

C. Paul wrote that God is longsuffering.

Romans 2:4, *Or do you despise the riches of His goodness, forbearance, and longsuffering, not knowing that the goodness of God leads you to repentance?*

Romans 9:22, *What if God, wanting to show His wrath and to make His power known, endured with much longsuffering the vessels of wrath prepared for destruction.*

D. "Gentleness" may also be translated as "kindness" when speaking about the nature of God.

Ephesians 2:7, *That in the ages to come He might show the exceeding riches of His grace in His kindness toward us in Christ Jesus.*

Titus 3:4, *But when the kindness and the love of God our Savior toward man appeared. . .*

Matthew 11:29, *"Take My yoke upon you and learn from Me, for I am gentle and lowly in heart, and you will find rest for your souls."*

3. THE INTERRELATIONSHIP OF THE FRUIT OF THE SPIRIT

A. I Timothy 6:11, *But you, O man of God, flee these things and pursue righteousness, godliness, faith, love, patience, gentleness.*

B. Romans 14:17, *For the kingdom of God is not food and drink, but righteousness and peace and joy in the Holy Spirit.*

C. Romans 15:13, *Now may the God of hope fill you with all joy and peace in believing, that you may abound in hope by the power of the Holy Spirit.*

D. Ephesians 4:1-3, *I, therefore, the prisoner of the Lord, beseech you to walk worthy of the calling with which you were called,*

v. 2, *with all lowliness and gentleness, with longsuffering, bearing with one another in love,*

v. 3, *endeavoring to keep the unity of the Spirit in the bond of peace.*

E. II Corinthians 6:4-6, *But in all things we commend ourselves as ministers of God: in much patience, in tribulations, in needs, in distresses,*

v. 5, *in stripes, in imprisonments, in tumults, in labors, in sleeplessness, in fastings;*

v. 6, *by purity, by knowledge, by longsuffering, by kindness, by the Holy Spirit, by sincere love.*

F. II Timothy 3:10-11, *But you have carefully followed my doctrine, manner of life, purpose, faith, longsuffering, love, perseverance,*

v. 11, *persecutions, afflictions, which happened to me at Antioch, at Iconium, at Lystra—what persecutions I endured. And out of them all the Lord delivered me.*

G. Hebrews 6:12, *That you do not become sluggish, but imitate those who through faith and patience inherit the promises.*

H. II Thessalonians 1:11, *Therefore we also pray always for you that our God would count you worthy of this calling, and fulfill all the good pleasure of His goodness and the work of faith with power.*

I. I Thessalonians 5:8, *But let us who are of the day be sober, putting on the breastplate of faith and love, and as a helmet the hope of salvation.*

J. I Timothy 4:12, *Let no one despise your youth, but be an example to the believers in word, in conduct, in love, in spirit, in faith, in purity.*

K. Revelation 2:19, *"I know your works, love, service, faith, and your patience; and as for your works, the last are more than the first."*

L. I Corinthians 4:21, *What do you want? Shall I come to you with a rod, or in love and a spirit of gentleness?*

M. II Peter 1:5-7, *But also for this very reason, giving all diligence, add to your faith virtue, to virtue knowledge,*

v. 6, *to knowledge self-control, to self-control perseverance, to perseverance godliness,*

v. 7, *to godliness brotherly kindness, and to brotherly kindness love.*

4. WE ARE KNOWN BY OUR FRUIT

A. Though the gifts of the Holy Spirit are important, Paul taught that they do not necessarily prove our relationship to Jesus. The Corinthian church, to whom Paul taught about the gifts, had to be reproved for many carnal things (including adultery). Paul said that he could not even address them as spiritual people.

I Corinthians 3:1, *And I, brethren, could not speak to you as to spiritual people but as to carnal, as to babes in Christ.*

B. A friend of mine met a young man returning from an illicit affair with a prostitute and corrected him for his conduct. The boy's response was, "I can still speak in tongues." If the gifts are not backed by a holy life which produces the fruit of the Spirit, they are void and useless.

C. Matthew 7:16-23, *"You will know them by their fruits. Do men gather grapes from thornbushes or figs from thistles?*

v. 17, *"Even so, every good tree bears good fruit, but a bad tree bears bad fruit.*

v. 18, *"A good tree cannot bear bad fruit, nor can a bad tree bear good fruit.*

v. 19, *"Every tree that does not bear good fruit is cut down and thrown into the fire.*

v. 20, *"Therefore by their fruits you will know them.*

v. 21, *"Not everyone who says to Me, 'Lord, Lord,' shall enter the kingdom of heaven, but he who does the will of My Father in heaven.*

v. 22, *"Many will say to Me in that day, 'Lord, Lord, have we not prophesied in Your name, cast out demons in Your name, and done many wonders in Your name?'*

v. 23, *"And then I will declare to them, 'I never knew you; depart from Me, you who practice lawlessness!' "*

D. Galatians 5:5, 13, 16-18, *For we through the Spirit eagerly wait for the hope of righteousness by faith.*

v. 13, *For you, brethren, have been called to liberty; only do not use liberty as an opportunity for the flesh, but through love serve one another.*

v. 16, *I say then: Walk in the Spirit, and you shall not fulfill the lust of the flesh.*

v. 17, *For the flesh lusts against the Spirit, and the Spirit against the flesh; and these are contrary to one another, so that you do not do the things that you wish.*

v. 18, *But if you are led by the Spirit, you are not under the law.*

5. THE DEVIL WANTS YOU IN BONDAGE

He cries out for circumcision of the flesh.

Galatians 6:12, *As many as desire to make a good showing in the flesh, these would compel you to be circumcised, only that they may not suffer persecution for the cross of Christ.*

NOTES

_____

_____

_____

_____

_____

_____

_____

_____

_____

_____

_____

_____

_____

_____

_____

_____

_____

_____

_____

_____

_____

_____

_____

_____

_____

_____

_____

_____

_____

_____

_____

_____

_____

_____

_____

THE PERSON OF
THE HOLY SPIRIT

Lesson 19

THE PERSON OF THE HOLY SPIRIT
AND THE APOSTLE PAUL

INTRODUCTION

Few people have had as great an experience with the Person of the Holy Spirit as the apostle Paul.

READING

Acts 16:6-7, *Now when they had gone through Phrygia and the region of Galatia, they were forbidden by the Holy Spirit to preach the word in Asia.*

v. 7, *After they had come to Mysia, they tried to go into Bithynia, but the Spirit did not permit them.*

1. PAUL WAS ARRESTED BY THE SPIRIT

Paul was knocked down by the Holy Spirit at Damascus.

Acts 9:3-4, *As he journeyed he came near Damascus, and suddenly a light shone around him from heaven.*

v. 4, *Then he fell to the ground, and heard a voice saying to him, "Saul, Saul, why are you persecuting Me?"*

2. PAUL WAS FILLED WITH THE SPIRIT

Paul received the Holy Spirit immediately after his conversion.

Acts 9:17-18, *And Ananias went his way and entered the house; and laying his hands on him he said, "Brother Saul, the Lord Jesus, who appeared to you on the road as you came, has sent me that you may receive your sight and be filled with the Holy Spirit."*

v. 18, *Immediately there fell from his eyes something like scales, and he received his sight at once; and he arose and was baptized.*

3. PAUL BECAME AN APOSTLE BY THE HOLY SPIRIT

The Holy Spirit made Paul an apostle.

Romans 1:1, *Paul, a servant of Jesus Christ, called to be an apostle, separated to the gospel of God.*

4. PAUL WAS TAUGHT BY THE HOLY SPIRIT

Paul was dramatically and remarkably given divine revelation from the Person of the Holy Spirit.

Galatians 1:11-18, *But I make known to you, brethren, that the gospel which was preached by me is not according to man.*

v. 12, *For I neither received it from man, nor was I taught it, but it came through the revelation of Jesus Christ.*

v. 13, *For you have heard of my former conduct in Judaism, how I persecuted the church of God beyond measure and tried to destroy it.*

v. 14, *And I advanced in Judaism beyond many of my contemporaries in my own nation, being more exceedingly zealous for the traditions of my fathers.*

v. 15, *But when it pleased God, who separated me from my mother's womb and called me through His grace,*

v. 16. *to reveal His Son in me, that I might preach Him among the Gentiles, I did not immediately confer with flesh and blood,*

v. 17. *nor did I go up to Jerusalem to those who were apostles before me; but I went to Arabia, and returned again to Damascus.*

v. 18, *Then after three years I went up to Jerusalem to see Peter, and remained with him fifteen days.*

5. PAUL TAUGHT ABOUT THE HOLY SPIRIT

Paul taught people how to live in the Holy Spirit.

Galatians 3:2-3, 5, *This only I want to learn from you: Did you receive the Spirit by the works of the law, or by the hearing of faith?*

v. 3, *Are you so foolish? Having begun in the Spirit, are you now being made perfect by the flesh?*

v. 5, *Therefore He who supplies the Spirit to you and works miracles among you, does He do it by the works of the law, or by the hearing of faith?*

6. PAUL WAS LED BY THE PERSON OF THE HOLY SPIRIT

The Spirit commanded him to go to Macedonia.

Acts 16:9-10, *And a vision appeared to Paul in the night. A man of Macedonia stood and pleaded with him, saying, "Come over to Macedonia and help us."*

v. 10, *Now after he had seen the vision, immediately we sought to go to Macedonia, concluding that the Lord had called us to preach the gospel to them.*

7. PAUL TAUGHT THE TRUTH ABOUT THE GIFTS OF THE HOLY SPIRIT

A. Paul outlined the gifts of the Spirit and their ministry.

I Corinthians 12:4-11, 28, *Now there are diversities of gifts, but the same Spirit.*

v. 5, *There are differences of ministries, but the same Lord.*

v. 6, *And there are diversities of activities, but it is the same God who works all in all.*

v. 7, *But the manifestation of the Spirit is given to each one for the profit of all:*

v. 8, *for to one is given the word of wisdom through the Spirit, to another the word of knowledge through the same Spirit,*

v. 9, *to another faith by the same Spirit, to another gifts of healings by the same Spirit,*

v. 10, *to another the working of miracles, to another prophecy, to another discerning of spirits, to another different kinds of tongues, to another the interpretation of tongues.*

v. 11, *But one and the same Spirit works all these things, distributing to each one individually as He wills.*

v. 28, *And God has appointed these in the church: first apostles, second prophets, third teachers, after that miracles, then gifts of healings, helps, administrations, varieties of tongues.*

B. Paul cautioned the Church that to be beneficial the gifts must operate in love.

I Corinthians 13:1-3, *Though I speak with the tongues of men and of angels, but have not love, I have become sounding brass or a clanging cymbal.*

v. 2, *And though I have the gift of prophecy, and understand all mysteries and all knowledge, and though I have all faith, so that I could remove mountains, but have not love, I am nothing.*

v. 3, *And though I bestow all my goods to feed the poor, and though I give my body to be burned, but have not love, it profits me nothing.*

8. PAUL KNEW THE WAY OF THE HOLY SPIRIT

I Thessalonians 1:5, *For our gospel did not come to you in word only, but also in power, and in the Holy Spirit and in much assurance, as you know what kind of men we were among you for your sake.*

NOTES

_____

_____

_____

_____

_____

_____

_____

_____

_____

_____

_____

_____

_____

_____

_____

_____

_____

_____

_____

_____

_____

_____

_____

_____

_____

_____

_____

_____

_____

_____

_____

_____

THE PERSON OF
THE HOLY SPIRIT

Lesson 20

THE PERSON OF THE HOLY SPIRIT
IN ROMANS EIGHT

INTRODUCTION

Romans chapter eight teaches about the function and operation of the Holy Spirit in relationship with the believer.

There are 12 functions and operations of the Holy Spirit listed in Romans eight. In this chapter, the Holy Spirit is mentioned 18 times. He is mentioned only twice in the first seven chapters of Romans.

READING

Romans 8:18-19, *For I consider that the sufferings of this present time are not worthy to be compared with the glory which shall be revealed in us.*

v. 19, *For the earnest expectation of the creation eagerly waits for the revealing of the sons of God.*

1. WALK AFTER THE SPIRIT

    A. The Holy Spirit has a walk. Following Him rids the believer of condemnation.

Romans 8:1, *There is therefore now no condemnation to those who are in Christ Jesus, who do not walk according to the flesh, but according to the Spirit.*

B. The Holy Spirit has a philosophy.

Romans 8:28, *And we know that all things work together for good to those who love God, to those who are the called according to His purpose.*

2. THE LAW OF THE SPIRIT OF LIFE

A. The law of the Spirit canceled the penalty of death.

Romans 8:2-3, *For the law of the Spirit of life in Christ Jesus has made me free from the law of sin and death.*

v. 3, *For what the law could not do in that it was weak through the flesh, God did by sending His own Son in the likeness of sinful flesh, on account of sin: He condemned sin in the flesh.*

B. The law of the Spirit fulfilled all righteousness.

Romans 8:4, *That the righteous requirement of the law might be fulfilled in us who do not walk according to the flesh but according to the Spirit.*

1) The Holy Spirit has a law–the law of life.

2) It is life in Christ–not righteousness.

3) It is opposite of the laws of sin and death.

3. OBEDIENT TO A MASTER

You will obey your master, whether evil or good.

Romans 8:5, *For those who live according to the flesh set their minds on the things of the flesh, but those who live according to the Spirit, the things of the Spirit.*

4. THE HOLY SPIRIT DWELLS WITHIN US

A. He lives inside the born-again person.

Romans 8:16, *The Spirit Himself bears witness with our spirit that we are children of God.*

B. He does not just visit the believer, He resides within him!

Romans 8:9, *But you are not in the flesh but in the Spirit, if indeed the Spirit of God dwells in you. Now if anyone does not have the Spirit of Christ, he is not His.*

5. THE HOLY SPIRIT IS THE SPIRIT OF LIFE

A. Sin is death, or separation, from God.

Romans 8:10, *And if Christ is in you, the body is dead because of sin, but the Spirit is life because of righteousness.*

B. The prodigal son was declared dead when he was away from the father.

Luke 15:24, *"For this my son was dead and is alive again; he was lost and is found.' And they began to be merry."*

6. HE IS THE SPIRIT OF RESURRECTION

A. The Holy Spirit activated the inanimate corpse of Jesus of Nazareth in the grave, breathed upon it, and caused immortality to give it life!

B. The same Holy Spirit, who overshadowed Mary and caused her to conceive and give birth to a Son named Jesus, also caused Christ to rise from the grave.

Romans 8:11, *But if the Spirit of Him who raised Jesus from the dead dwells in you, He who raised Christ from the dead will also give life to your mortal bodies through His Spirit who dwells in you.*

What a revelation!

7. WE MORTIFY THE DEEDS OF THE BODY THROUGH THE SPIRIT

The power of the Holy Spirit enables the believer to actually kill and destroy, or mortify, the flesh.

Romans 8:13, *For if you live according to the flesh you will die; but if by the Spirit you put to death the deeds of the body, you will live.*

8. WE ARE LED BY THE SPIRIT OF GOD

The Holy Spirit is aggressive in the believer. He leads; we follow.

Romans 8:14, *For as many as are led by the Spirit of God, these are sons of God.*

9. THE SPIRIT OF ADOPTION

We are not only servants of God, but through spiritual rebirth, we actually become His legitimate children with all the benefits of a blood relationship. The Holy Spirit gives us this assurance, this inward knowledge. He bears witness.

Romans 8:15, *For you did not receive the spirit of bondage again to fear, but you received the Spirit of adoption by whom we cry out, "Abba, Father."*

10. THE FIRST FRUITS OF THE HOLY SPIRIT

On this earth, we receive the beginning of our inheritance through anointing, joy, rejoicing and answered prayers.

Romans 8:23, *And not only they, but we also who have the firstfruits of the Spirit, even we ourselves groan within ourselves, eagerly waiting for the adoption, the redemption of our body.*

11. THE SPIRIT HELPS OUR INFIRMITIES

The Spirit makes intercession for us. When our minds do not know what to say, the Holy Spirit speaks through us.

Romans 8:26, *Likewise the Spirit also helps in our weaknesses. For we do not know what we should pray for as we ought, but the Spirit Himself makes intercession for us with groanings which cannot be uttered.*

12. THE MIND OF THE SPIRIT

Only the born-again person may possess an understanding of the mind of the Spirit.

The Holy Spirit possesses the powers of intercession to speak to the Father and Son on behalf of believers.

Romans 8:27, *Now He who searches the hearts knows what the mind of the Spirit is, because He makes intercession for the saints according to the will of God.*

NOTES

THE PERSON OF
THE HOLY SPIRIT

Lesson 21

THE HOLY SPIRIT IN THE BOOK OF REVELATION

INTRODUCTION

Genesis is the Alpha and Revelation is the Omega of truth about the Holy Spirit. The Holy Spirit speaks to the churches throughout the Bible. The ultimate revelation to man is deeply involved with the function and operation of the Person of the Holy Spirit.

READING

Revelation 3:13, *"He who has an ear, let him hear what the Spirit says to the churches."*

1. IN THE SPIRIT ON THE LORD'S DAY

Revelation 1:10, *I was in the Spirit on the Lord's Day, and I heard behind me a loud voice, as of a trumpet.*

2. SEVEN-FOLD HOLY SPIRIT

The seven Spirits before the throne represent the Third Person of the Trinity in the fullness and completeness of divine illumination and energy.

Revelation 4:5, *And from the throne proceeded lightnings, thunderings, and voices. And there were seven lamps of fire burning before the throne, which are the seven Spirits of God.*

Revelation 5:6, *And I looked, and behold, in the midst of the throne and of the four living creatures, and in the midst of the elders, stood a Lamb as though it had been slain, having seven horns and seven eyes, which are the seven Spirits of God sent out into all the earth.*

3. THE HOLY SPIRIT REVEALED OUR ETERNAL HOME

The New Jerusalem descends from God out of heaven.

Revelation 21:10, *And he carried me away in the Spirit to a great and high mountain, and showed me the great city, the holy Jerusalem, descending out of heaven from God.*

4. A FINAL BIBLICAL APPEAL FROM THE HOLY SPIRIT

The Holy Spirit calls men to Christ.

Revelation 22:17, *And the Spirit and the bride say, "Come!" And let him who hears say, "Come!" And let him who thirsts come. And whoever desires, let him take the water of life freely.*

A. The Holy Spirit cries, "Come."

B. The Bride, or Church cries, "Come."

    1) All who hear can come.

    2) The thirsty can come.

    3) Whosoever desires may come to the water of life.

5. SEVEN DIFFERENT THINGS TO SEVEN DIFFERENT CHURCHES

A. Ephesus

God knows our works. We do not need to remind Him about our good deeds.

Revelation 2:2, *I know your works, your labor, your patience, and that you cannot bear those who are evil. And you have tested those who say they are apostles and are not, and have found them liars.*

B. Smyrna

The first death is separation from our environment, but the second death is separation from God.

Revelation 2:11, *He who has an ear, let him hear what the Spirit says to the churches. He who overcomes shall not be hurt by the second death.*

C. Pergamos

God has prepared a wonderful future for the overcomer. Even our names will be changed.

Revelation 2:17, *He who has an ear, let him hear what the Spirit says to the churches. To him who overcomes I will give some of the hidden manna to eat. And I will give him a white stone, and on the stone a new name written which no one knows except him who receives it.*

D. Thyatira

Our reign will be a glorious one, symbolized not only by authority, but also by a star.

Revelation 2:26-28, *And he who overcomes, and keeps My works until the end, to him I will give power over the nations—*

v. 27, *"He shall rule them with a rod of iron; As the potter's vessels shall be broken to pieces"—as I also have received from My Father;*

v. 28, *and I will give him the morning star.*

E. Sardis

God will recognize us as His heirs with all rights and privileges.

Revelation 3:5, *"He who overcomes shall be clothed in white garments, and I will not blot out his name from the Book of Life; but I will confess his name before My Father and before His angels."*

F. Philadelphia

We will have a permanent dwelling with God and receive His seal.

Revelation 3:12, *He who overcomes, I will make him a pillar in the temple of My God, and he shall go out no more. And I will write on him the name of My God and the name of the city of My God, the New Jerusalem, which comes down out of heaven from My God. And I will write on him My new name.*

G. Laodicea

The victor, or overcomer, will sit on the throne with Jesus.

Revelation 3:21, *To him who overcomes I will grant to sit with Me on My throne, as I also overcame and sat down with My Father on His throne.*

STUDY GUIDE

INDIANA CHRISTIAN UNIVERSITY

THE PERSON OF THE HOLY SPIRIT

Lesson 22

HOW TO KNOW AND RECEIVE THE PERSON OF THE HOLY SPIRIT

INTRODUCTION

This subject is so important that fasting and prayer are often needed. Yet it can be explained so simply that even little children can understand it.

READING

Acts 1:8, *"But you shall receive power when the Holy Spirit has come upon you; and you shall be witnesses to Me in Jerusalem, and in all Judea and Samaria, and to the end of the earth."*

1. YOU RECEIVE THE HOLY SPIRIT AT CONVERSION

A. Every believer is born of the Spirit.

John 3:6-8, *"That which is born of the flesh is flesh, and that which is born of the Spirit is spirit.*

v. 7, *"Do not marvel that I said to you, 'You must be born again.'*

v. 8, *"The wind blows where it wishes, and you hear the sound of it, but cannot tell where it comes from and where it goes. So is everyone who is born of the Spirit."*

B. This is a new realm for the natural man. The Holy Spirit's throne is the human belly.

John 7:38-39, *"He who believes in Me, as the Scripture has said, out of his heart will flow rivers of living water."*

v. 39, *But this He spoke concerning the Spirit, whom those believing in Him would receive; for the Holy Spirit was not yet given, because Jesus was not yet glorified.*

2. BELIEVERS CAN ASK FOR THE HOLY SPIRIT

You must ask in faith and deep integrity.

Luke 11:13, *"If you then, being evil, know how to give good gifts to your children, how much more will your heavenly Father give the Holy Spirit to those who ask Him!"*

3. THE DISCIPLES RECEIVED THE HOLY SPIRIT ON THE DAY OF PENTECOST

A. They received after waiting on the Lord in the Upper Room for ten days.

Acts 2:1-4, *Now when the Day of Pentecost had fully come, they were all with one accord in one place.*

v. 2, *And suddenly there came a sound from heaven, as of a rushing mighty wind, and it filled the whole house where they were sitting.*

v. 3, *Then there appeared to them divided tongues, as of fire, and one sat upon each of them.*

v. 4, *And they were all filled with the Holy Spirit and began to speak with other tongues, as the Spirit gave them utterance.*

B. Their waiting was an act of obedience to Christ.

Luke 24:49, *"Behold, I send the Promise of My Father upon you; but tarry in the city of Jerusalem until you are endued with power from on high."*

4. RECEIVE THROUGH THE LAYING ON OF HANDS

A. The Spirit of God can be transmitted by personal contact from a Spirit-filled believer to one who is not.

I Timothy 4:14, *Do not neglect the gift that is in you, which was given to you by prophecy with the laying on of the hands of the presbytery.*

II Timothy 1:6, *Therefore I remind you to stir up the gift of God which is in you through the laying on of my hands.*

B. In the Old Testament, the Spirit in one prophet could be transmitted to another through the laying on of hands.

Deuteronomy 34:8-9, *And the children of Israel wept for Moses in the plains of Moab thirty days. So the days of weeping and mourning for Moses ended.*

v. 9, *Now Joshua the son of Nun was full of the spirit of wisdom, for Moses had laid his hands on him; so the children of Israel heeded him, and did as the LORD had commanded Moses.*

C. In the New Testament, Ananias laid hands on Saul of Tarsus.

Acts 9:17, *And Ananias went his way and entered the house; and laying his hands on him he said, "Brother Saul, the Lord Jesus, who appeared to you on the road as you came, has sent me that you may receive your sight and be filled with the Holy Spirit."*

5. THE HOLY SPIRIT AND YOU

A. You can hear the Holy Spirit.

B. You can follow the Holy Spirit.

C. You can understand the will of God through the Holy Spirit.

D. You can obey the Holy Spirit.

INDIANA CHRISTIAN UNIVERSITY
CORRESPONDENCE COURSE INSTRUCTIONS

INDIVIDUAL STUDY

The courses offered are directed to meet the practical needs of today's Christian. The following steps should be considered in beginning your study.

1. Read each lesson of the study guide carefully.

2. Listen to the tapes carefully. They will explain the course content and clarify what you may not understand from the written lesson.

3. Read the lessons and listen to the tapes in the way most helpful to you. It is suggested you read the lesson once, listen to the tape, and then read the lesson again.

4. It is recommended that you complete each course within eight weeks.

5. At the completion of each course, a test should be completed and mailed to the school so that you may earn a certificate of credit. Send $10 for grading costs along with your completed test.

6. You may also obtain college credit for the course you have completed by submitting a term paper on a topic related to your course. The papers should be 10 to 12 double-spaced typewritten pages. All information from source material must be properly footnoted and the sources must be listed in a bibliography. For further instruction on term paper form, please check any standard college English text book. An instruction manual on term paper writing is available from Indiana Christian University (Box 12, South Bend, IN 46624) for $1 plus 50¢ postage and handling. Five source books must be used in writing the paper.

GROUP STUDY

Groups wishing to study correspondence together should have a qualified individual to teach the group. These courses can be used for pastors' studies or for home prayer and Bible study groups. It is recommended that a videotape be used in the area of group study.

Further information concerning availability of materials, costs, etc., may be obtained by writing to the school.

....

NAME_____

ADDRESS _____

CITY _____STATE _____ ZIP _____

Name of completed course: _____

Course number:_____Date completed: _____

Mail this form, with test to:

Indiana Christian University
P.O. Box 12
South Bend, IN 46624

For office use only:
Graded by:_____ Score: _____ Date certificate mailed: _____

STUDY GUIDE

INDIANA CHRISTIAN UNIVERSITY

THE PERSON OF
THE HOLY SPIRIT

TEST

INSTRUCTIONS: You may not use your study guide or any notes. You may refer to your Bible, but only the biblical text (not the margins, footnotes, concordance or editorial materials).

1. The Bible is the _____ source of information on the Third Person of the Trinity.
   - ❏ A. Recommended
   - ❏ B. Best
   - ❏ C. Most complete
   - ❏ D. Sole

2. The Holy Spirit has a _____ made up of mind, will and emotions.
   - ❏ A. Body
   - ❏ B. Soul
   - ❏ C. Spirit
   - ❏ D. None of the above

3. The Holy Spirit should always be spoken of as _____.
   - ❏ A. He
   - ❏ B. She
   - ❏ C. It
   - ❏ D. All of the above

4. Man's salvation is through _____.
   - ❏ A. Water
   - ❏ B. Blood
   - ❏ C. Spirit
   - ❏ D. All of the above

5. The Holy Spirit proceeds from _____.
   - ❏ A. The Father
   - ❏ B. The Son
   - ❏ C. Both A and B
   - ❏ D. Neither A nor B

6. Who was indwelt by the Spirit without measure?
   - ❏ A. John the Baptist
   - ❏ B. Paul
   - ❏ C. Moses
   - ❏ D. Christ

True/False

T F

7. ☐ ☐ The Holy Spirit searches only the things we ask Him to investigate.

8. ☐ ☐ The Holy Spirit seals believers for redemption.

9. ☐ ☐ The Holy Spirit is omniscient, omnipotent and unsearchable.

10. ☐ ☐ The sin against the Holy Spirit is backsliding.

11. ☐ ☐ Before chapter eight of Romans, the Holy Spirit is mentioned twice; He is mentioned 18 times in this one chapter.

12-14. List three of the five roles (jobs He performs or positions He holds) of the Holy Spirit.

12. _____

13. _____

14. _____

15-18. List four of the five enemies of the Holy Spirit.

15. _____

16. _____

17. _____

18. _____

19-24. List six phases of the operation of the Holy Spirit in the life of Jesus.

19. _____

20. _____

21. _____

22. _____

23. _____

24. _____

25-27. List three of the five "Paraclete statements" about the Holy Spirit.

25. _____

26. _____

27. _____

28-30. List the three reproofs or convictions of the Holy Spirit.

28. _____

29. _____

30. _____

31-39. List the nine fruit of the Spirit.

31. _____

32. _____

33. _____

34. _____

35. _____

36. _____

37. _____

38. _____

39. _____

40-43. List four of the six ways to receive the power of the Spirit.

40. _____

41. _____

42. _____

43. _____

44-46. List the gifts of power.

44. _____

45. _____

46. _____

47-49. List the gifts of revelation.

47. _____

48. _____

49. _____

50-52. List the gifts of inspiration.

50. _____

51. _____

52. _____

53-60. List eight of the twelve functions of the Holy Spirit listed in Romans chapter eight.

53. _____

54. _____

55. _____

56. _____

57. _____

58. _____

59. _____

60. _____

61-100. Fill in the blanks of these Bible verses about the Holy Spirit.

61. God is Spirit, and those who worship Him must worship in spirit and _____.

62. Nevertheless I tell you the truth. It is to your advantage that I go away; for if I do not go away, the _____ will not come to you; but if I depart, I will send Him to you.

63. For there are three that bear witness in heaven: the Father, the Word, and the Holy Spirit; and these three are _____.

64. Now He who searches the hearts knows what the mind of the Spirit is, because He makes _____ for the saints according to the will of God.

65. By this you know the Spirit of God: Every spirit that confesses that Jesus Christ has come in the _____ is of God.

66. However, when He, the Spirit of _____, has come, He will guide you into all truth; for He will not speak on His own authority, but whatever He hears He will speak; and He will tell you things to come.

67. But you shall receive_____when the Holy Spirit has come upon you; and you shall be witnesses to Me in Jerusalem, and in all Judea and Samaria, and to the end of the earth.

68. But if the Spirit of Him who raised Jesus from the dead dwells in you, He who raised Christ from the dead will also _____your mortal bodies through His Spirit who dwells in you.

69. For as many as are _____ by the Spirit of God, these are sons of God.

70. And take the helmet of salvation, and the _____of the Spirit, which is the word of God.

71. Now I beg you, brethren, through the Lord Jesus Christ, and through the _____ of the Spirit, that you strive together with me in prayers to God for me.

72. For the kingdom of God is not eating and drinking, but righteousness and peace and _____ in the Holy Spirit.

73. Likewise the Spirit also helps in our_____. For we do not know what we should pray for as we ought, but the Spirit Himself makes intercession for us with groanings which cannot be uttered.

74. How God_____Jesus of Nazareth with the Holy Spirit and with power, who went about doing good and healing all who were oppressed by the devil, for God was with Him.

75. When He had been baptized, Jesus came up immediately from the water; and behold, the heavens were opened to Him, and He saw the Spirit of God descending like a _____ and alighting upon Him.

76. But you are not in the flesh but in the Spirit, if indeed the Spirit of God dwells in you. Now if anyone does not have the Spirit of Christ, he is _____ His.

77. The grace of the Lord Jesus Christ, and the love of God, and the _____ of the Holy Spirit be with you all. Amen.

78. Go therefore and make disciples of all the nations, _____ them in the name of the Father and of the Son and of the Holy Spirit.

79. It is the Spirit who gives life; the _____ profits nothing. The words that I speak to you are spirit, and they are life.

80. In Him you also trusted, after you heard the word of truth, the gospel of your salvation; in whom also, having believed, you were sealed with the Holy Spirit of promise_____.

81. And do not _____ the Holy Spirit of God, by whom you were sealed for the day of redemption.

82. How much more shall the blood of Christ, who through the _____ Spirit offered Himself without spot to God, cleanse your conscience from dead works to serve the living God?

83. Now may the God of hope fill you with all joy and peace in believing, that you may abound in _____ by the power of the Holy Spirit.

84. Jesus answered, "Most assuredly, I say to you, unless one is _____ of water and the Spirit, he cannot enter the kingdom of God."

85. Or do you not know that your body is the_____ of the Holy Spirit who is in you, whom you have from God, and you are not your own?

86. And if Christ is in you, the body is dead because of sin, but the Spirit is life because of _____.

87. Who also made us sufficient as ministers of the new covenant, not of the letter but of the Spirit; for the_____kills, but the Spirit gives life.

88. And I will pray the Father, and He will give you another Helper, that He may abide with you _____.

89. I say then: _____ in the Spirit, and you shall not fulfill the lust of the flesh.

90. Now concerning spiritual gifts, brethren, I do not want you to be _____.

91. Therefore I say to you, every sin and _____ will be forgiven men, but the _____ against the Spirit will not be forgiven men.

92. And the Spirit and the _____ say, "Come!" And let him who hears say, "Come!"

93. And it shall come to pass in the last days, says God, That I will pour out of My Spirit on_____ flesh.

94. But if I cast out demons by the Spirit of God, surely the _____ of God has come upon you.

95. And when they had prayed, the place where they were assembled together was shaken; and they were all filled with the Holy Spirit, and they spoke the word of God with _____.

96. And my speech and my preaching were not with persuasive words of human wisdom, but in _____ of the Spirit and of power.

97. For God has not given us a spirit of_____, but of power and of love and of a sound mind.

98. Therefore He who supplies the Spirit to you and works miracles among you, does He do it by the works of the law, or by the hearing of_____?

99. But you, beloved, building yourselves up on your most holy faith, _____ in the Holy Spirit.

100. But earnestly_____ the best gifts. And yet I show you a more excellent way.

6